Kabbalah and Exodus

By the same author:

Adam and the Kabbalistic Trees
A Kabbalistic Universe
The Way of Kabbalah
Introduction to The World of Kabbalah
The Kabbalist at Work
Kabbalah: School of the Soul
Psychology and Kabbalah
The Kabbalistic Tree of Life
Kabbalah and Astrology
The Anointed—*a Kabbalistic novel*
The Anatomy of Fate
The Path of a Kabbalist
Kabbalistic Contemplations

By Other Publishers:

Kabbalah—The Divine Plan (*HarperCollins*)
Kabbalah, Tradition of Hidden Knowledge (*Thames & Hudson*)
Astrology, The Celestial Mirror (*Thames & Hudson*)
As Above So Below (*Stuart & Watkins*)

Kabbalah and Exodus

Z'ev ben Shimon Halevi

KS Books Ltd
London
This edition published by:

www.ksbooksltd.com
E-mail: info@ksbooksltd.com

First published in 1980 by Rider & Co.
Revised Edition in 2008 by Kabbalah Society
Copyright © Z'ev ben Shimon Halevi 1980, 2008, 2024

Every effort has been made to obtain permission to reproduce copyright material but there may be cases where we have been unable to trace the copyright holder. The publisher will be happy to correct any omissions in future printings.

The moral right of the author has been asserted.

All rights reserved.
No part of this publication may be reproduced, stored in a retrieval system or transmitted, in any form or by any means, without the prior permission in writing of the publisher, nor be circulated in any form of binding or cover other than that in which it is published and without a similar condition including this condition being imposed on the subsequent purchaser.

A CIP catalogue record for this book
is available from the British Library.

ISBN: 978-1-917606-17-2

Design by Lion Dickinson

Contents

	List of illustrations	viii
	Preface	xiii
	Introduction	xv
1.	General Kabbalistic Scheme	19

INCARNATION

2.	Prologue *Genesis*	35
3.	Bondage of Body *Exodus 1*	43
4.	Birth of Consciousness *Exodus 2*	48

SLEEP AND AWAKENING

5.	Initiation: Personal *Exodus 2*	53
6.	Moment of Grace *Exodus 3*	57
7.	Moment of Decision *Exodus 3–4*	62
8.	Moment of Hesitation *Exodus 4*	66

ACTION

9.	First Reaction *Exodus 5–6*	71
10.	Phenomena *Exodus 6–7*	74
11.	Physical Resistance *Exodus 8–9*	77
12.	Breakthrough *Exodus 10–12*	81
13.	Start of Journey *Exodus 13–14*	85
14.	Point of No Return *Exodus 14–15*	88

REBELLION AND RULES

15.	Regrets *Exodus 15–16*	95
16.	Beginning of Discipline *Exodus 16*	98
17.	Refreshment *Exodus 17*	102

18.	First Battle *Exodus 17*	105
19.	Teacher Taught *Exodus 18*	109

INITIATION

20.	Preparation *Exodus 19*	113
21.	Revelation *Exodus 19*	116
22.	Instruction on Divine *Exodus 20*	119
23.	Instruction on Man *Exodus 20*	122
24.	Rules *Exodus 20–23*	125
25.	Vision *Exodus 24*	129
26.	Ascent *Exodus 24*	132

KNOWLEDGE OF EXISTENCE

27.	Readiness *Exodus 25*	137
28.	Divinity *Exodus 25*	141
29.	Creation and Spirit *Exodus 25*	143
30.	Worlds within Worlds *Exodus 26*	146
31.	From Heaven to Earth *Exodus 27*	150

KNOWLEDGE OF MAN

32.	Human Hierarchy *Exodus 28*	157
33.	Levels in Man *Exodus 28*	160
34.	Degeneration of Knowledge *Exodus 29*	164
35.	Regeneration of Knowledge *Exodus 30–31*	167
36.	Day of Recreation *Exodus 31*	170

REVOLT

37.	Defection *Exodus 32*	175
38.	Inner Conflict *Exodus 32*	179
39.	Justice and Mercy *Exodus 32*	183
40.	Consequences *Exodus 32–33*	186

EXPERIENCE

41.	Illumination *Exodus 33*	192
42.	Enlightenment *Exodus 34*	195

| 43. | Radiance *Exodus 34* | 198 |

WORK

44.	Organisation and Direction *Exodus 35*	205
45.	Construction Work *Exodus 36*	208
46.	Architect *Exodus 37*	211
47.	Material and Skill *Exodus 38–39*	214
48.	Assembly and Consecration *Exodus 39–40*	217
	Epilogue	224
	Glossary	227
	Index	228

Illustrations

1.	The Burning Bush	x
2.	The Haggadah	xii
3.	Creation	xiv
4.	Origins	xvii
5.	Tree of Life	xviii
6.	Separation	20
7.	Four Worlds	22
8.	Jacob's Ladder	23
9.	Ezekiel's Vision	24
10.	Great Tree	26
11.	Body and Psyche	28
12.	Psyche in Detail	30
13.	Biblical Ladder	34
14.	Ark	37
15.	Melchizedek	38
16.	Jacob's Dream	41
17.	Descent	44
18.	Bondage	46
19.	Ladder of Moses	58
20.	Destiny	63
21.	Knowledge	75
22.	Ten Plagues	78
23.	Angel of Death	83
24.	Pillars of Fire and Smoke	90
25.	Manna from Heaven	99
26.	Battle	104
27.	Exodus	106
28.	The Teaching	112
29.	Ten Commandments	118
30.	Ladder of Mount Sinai	128
31.	Tribes	138
32.	Menorah	144

33.	Tabernacle Layout	148
34.	Tabernacle Ladder	152
35.	Hierarchy	156
36.	Regression	174
37.	The Pentateuch	180
38.	Places	187
39.	Enlightenment	200
40.	Priesthood	218

x

Figure 1—THE BURNING BUSH
Here Moses has a moment of illumination. This can happen to any individual. It is usually a life-challenging experience. In Moses's case it is the call to take on the destiny for which he has long and unknowingly been trained. Whether he takes up the task or not is a crucial act of free will. Each one of us has to face a crisis of this order at some time which determines our fate. (Rev.T. Bankes's Bible, 19th century.)

For Mosheh Rabbenu

Figure 2 — THE HAGGADAH
This book of the Passover contains the ceremony that celebrates the Exodus. Each participant is required to see themselves as actually being present at the time. According to Kabbalah, some individuals may well be old souls who were actually there, because the Tradition subscribes to the notion of reincarnation. This is called Gilgul, the Wheel of life and death. Note the Sefirot in this figure. (Dutch engraving, 17th century).

Preface

It is said that the scriptures contain the secret of Existence. Not many people perceive it, however, because they cannot see beyond the plain meaning of the words without the key of esoteric knowledge. This knowledge, called *Hokhmah Nestorah*, the Hidden Wisdom, transmitted by word of mouth down the ages from Abraham to the present day, is the esoteric framework upon which the Bible is based. Without this oral background, comprehension of the Divine Intention, the Universe's construction and mankind's purpose is impossible. Thus when the oral and written lines are interwoven, as they are in this work, the history of the Exodus becomes an analogue of an individual's escape from the physical bondage of the body, represented by Egypt, and his soul's struggle with psychological slavery in the desert as he strives to reach the Promised Land of the Spirit. In the Biblical, Talmudic and Kabbalistic accounts of the Israelites' outer journey, with its cosmic and individual dramas, are revealed the inner stages of initiation, trial and rebellion leading up to the realisation that the secret of Existence is that it is a mirror in which man reflects the Image of the Divine so that God may behold God.

LONDON, SPRING 5738 (1978)

Figure 3 — CREATION

These Seven Days mark, in Kabbalah, the second phase of manifestation as Existence unfolds. Here the symbolism speaks of the archetypes of the four Elements and the inhabitants of the Worlds that are coming into being. This is the level of Spirit, the essence of things which corresponds to Plato's realm of ideas. Above and beyond is the Divine World while below will be the Worlds of Form and Matter. Creation is where Time and the Divine plan emerge out of Eternity. (Rev.T. Bankes's Bible, 19th century).

Introduction

Ancient Jewish legend says that the Torah or Teaching existed before Creation and that God consulted it before bringing the Universe into being. This pre-Creation epoch is part of the oral tradition not included in the Bible canon and is therefore not generally known outside learned or esoteric circles.

The oral line goes on to say that when Adam and Eve were cast out of Eden, God had compassion upon them and sent the Archangel Raziel, whose name means Secrets of God, to give them a book. This volume, called the Book of Raziel, contained all the secrets of Existence. By it Adam could not only understand why he and the Universe existed but how to redeem his fallen state and fulfil his destiny.

The Book of Raziel was handed down to Seth, Adam's son, on to Enoch and then Noah. From here it was passed on to the anointed one of each generation until its contents were given to Abraham at his initiation by Melchizedek. This Knowledge was transmitted to Isaac, then Jacob who bestowed it upon Levi. Moses the Levite carried the spark of Knowledge until it burst into flame before the Burning Bush. After the revelation on Mount Sinai, where Moses was given the Complete Torah, he taught it to the Elders of Israel who have imparted it from that time on to the present day.

When the Torah came to be written down, traditionally in Moses's time, the Teaching was divided into what was called the Written and the Oral Laws. The former became the basis of the Bible and the latter the underlay of what was to become the Talmudic commentaries. The drafting of the Bible over many centuries was an esoteric operation requiring great knowledge and literary skill to contain the Teaching in what appears to be a collection of myths, family and tribal sagas, laws and poems. To the common-sense-minded the Bible is the history of the world and the Hebrew nation; to those who see it as allegory it is the analogue of cosmic and individual evolution; and to those who perceive it philosophically the Bible sets out the metaphysical scheme of Existence and the laws that govern mankind's spiritual development.

The Talmud is a vast rabbinical library of Biblical and sacred material not included in the written Torah. It ranges from regulations derived from canon law, through stories and practical and ethical advice to fragments of esoteric knowledge hinting at what still remains an oral tradition. This line of hidden wisdom has been passed from master to disciple over the centuries, producing different versions of the Teaching to suit various times and places. Nearly all the presentations, however, have been related to the scriptures as the Bible is considered the source of all mystical literature, especially in what came to be known as the study of *Pardes*. This term is composed of the initial letters of the Hebrew words for literal, allegorical, metaphysical and mystical interpretations of the Bible. The mystical approach is found in the classical kabbalistic work, the *Book of the Zohar*, produced, it is believed, by scholars in medieval Spain. The present work follows in the same tradition of *midrash* or investigation, in that it examines a Biblical text in terms of kabbalistic theory, ancient legend and contemporary knowledge so as to find what the scribes buried deep within the Book of Exodus.

Figure 4—ORIGINS
According to Kabbalah the Deity is beyond Existence. In order for God to behold God, there had to be a mirror. This came into being when the Absolute generated a space that would allow Existence to be. The three Hebrew words denote the No-thing-ness and the Limit-less-ness of God. The Fire of Divine Will encompasses the Ten Holy Numbers that emanate in a particular order. These Divine Principles will govern the three Worlds that will eventually emerge from this primal Realm of the Eternal. (Prof. James Russell, 20th century).

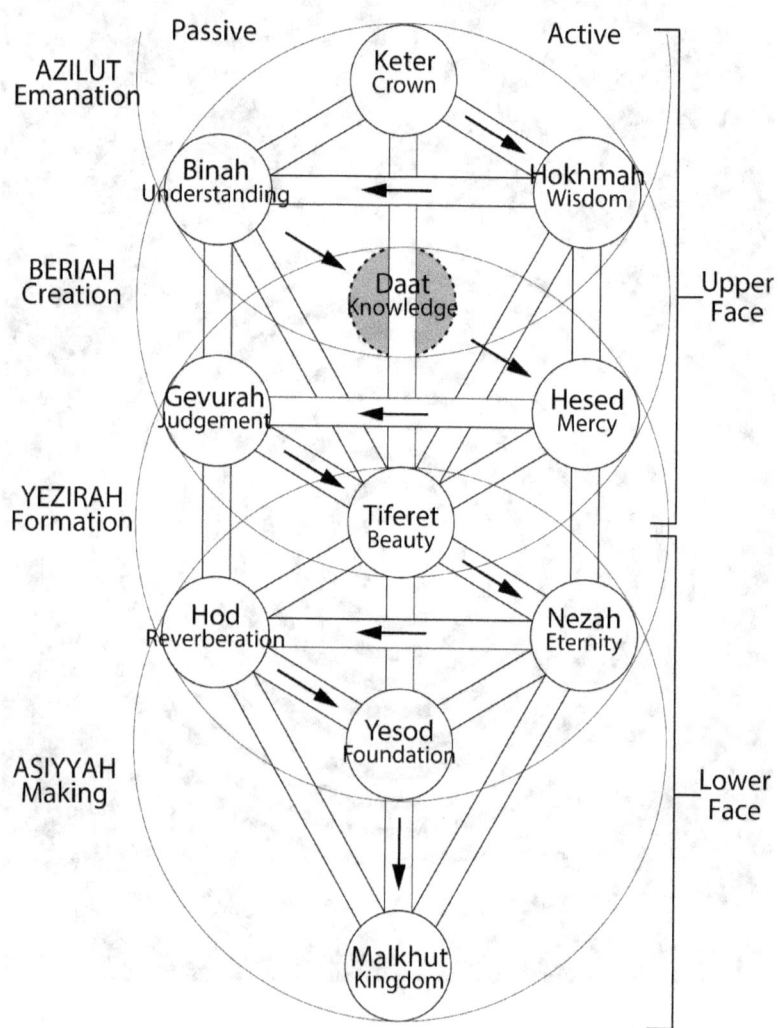

Figure 5—TREE OF LIFE
The Ten Sefirot, as they are called, are set out here in a classic diagram called the Tree of Life. They are linked in a specific way by the twenty-two paths of letters of the Hebrew Alefbet. These form, with the pillars, the kabbalistic metaphysical system which contains seven levels, a series of triads and what is called the Lightning Flash. The Tree also contains the origins of the four Worlds of Emanation, Creation, Formation and Action. The English translations are approximate as each sefirah has many aspects. (Halevi, 20th century).

1. General Kabbalistic Scheme

According to tradition, once there was only God. Nothing else existed. Kabbalah perceives the Godhead as AYIN or Absolute Nothing and AYIN SOF or Absolute All. Little else can be said because God is God and therefore totally alone and beyond human comprehension. Because of this, the oral tradition tells us, God wished to behold God and be known and so the mirror of Existence was called forth and man, the image of God, placed within it.

This process has been symbolically described in the following ways. Out of the midst of the Absolute there emerged a void, a dimensionless dot, as the Deity withdrew to allow a place in which Existence could be. Into this space there were spoken, according to some, Ten Divine Utterances that called Existence forth. Others see this act as the projection of Divine Will in the form of Light that emanated in ten stages from the Infinite to the finite. These stages of emanation successively define ten Divine Attributes which together form the Image of Divinity in manifestation; they are the sefirot, the instruments by which Existence is governed. Some mystics have seen this Image in the likeness of a primordial man, Adam Kadmon; others relate the Ten Attributes to each other in a more schematic way, known as the Tree of Life. They have also been perceived as a series of garments of Light concealing the Deity and some have called them the Glory of the ELOHIM.

This first manifestation of Existence is called, in Hebrew, the World of Azilut which means 'to be next to', or the World of Emanation. It is regarded as the perfect and unchanging realm of Eternity that precedes Creation. Here everything that is to be called forth, created, formed and made is held in potential for ever. As such it may be suspended until the Divine wishes Eternity to be dissolved back into nothingness again or wills creation to begin the process that will not finish until the End of Days when Adam, the image of God, will face and merge into the Divine again.

With the opening words of Genesis, 'In the beginning the ELOHIM created...' the unfolding of manifestation takes the next step towards

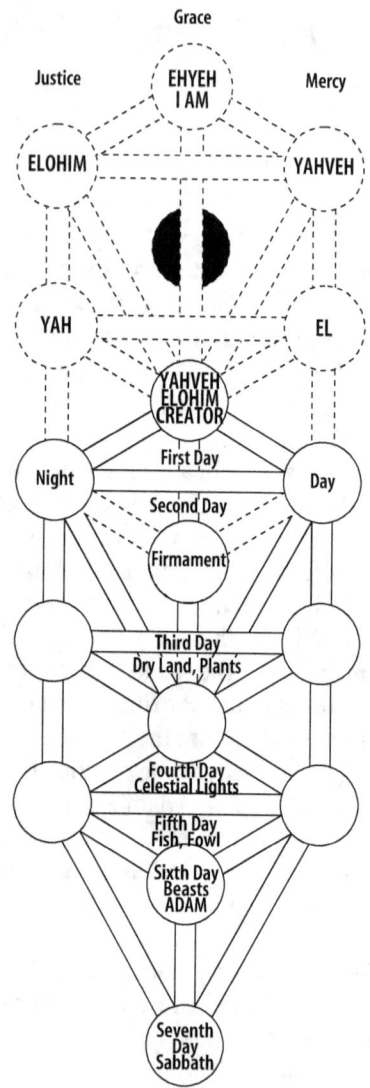

Figure 6—SEPARATION
Here the World of Creation emerges from the heart of the Divine Realm. This is the position of the Creator. This holy title is a combination of the two God names at the head of the two side columns. From here come the seven descending spiritual levels which later became the seven Heavens. Within this scheme is the Spiritual Universe and its inhabitants. The seventh Cosmic Day is when the Octave of Creation comes to rest. (Halevi, 20th century).

producing the three lower Worlds that are to emerge out of the eternal realm and into time and space. In the original Hebrew the use of a plural Name indicates the presence of the Divine Attributes of Azilut at work as they bring forth a second World in seven days or stages of creative manifestation. In the first chapter of Genesis the universe is separated from the Divine World and filled with different kinds of inhabitants. The last creature to be made is a second Adam who is *cidmutanu*, 'after Our likeness' the scripture says. On the final day of Creation the ELOHIM rests, having completed the cosmic World of Beriah, as it is called in Kabbalah. This World is seen as the spiritual counterpart to the Divine World of Emanation above and constitutes a second but lower Tree. The second chapter of Genesis then goes on to describe the next stage of manifestation as it moves away from its Source in the Infinite and the radiant World of the Sefirot.

A third World (or Tree), known in Kabbalah as Yezirah, then emerges out of Creation and is indicated by the operative word 'formed' used in Genesis 2:7 when, this time, YAHVEH-ELOHIM or the Merciful and Just God, called the Lord-God in the English translation, forms *ha Adam*, the man, out of dust and breathes into his nostrils a living soul. It was from here that Kabbalists took their concepts for the invisible aspects of a human being. In our scheme we use the term Spirit for that which relates to the Creative World of Heaven and Soul for the Formative World of Paradise or Eden. Out of Adam came Eve; that is, the united male and female parts of the Created Adam were separated and inhabited Eden as two entities where they enjoyed, besides the pleasures of the Garden, the privilege of free will. It is said by tradition that only mankind has the gift of free will because, being made in the image of God, the Deity granted them this privilege. However, with free will comes choice and therefore consequence. This law manifested after ignoring the instruction not to eat of the Tree of Knowledge which represented the presence of the World of Creation in Eden. When Adam and Eve ate of the apple they came into possession of Creative Knowledge and its enormous power for good or evil. Moreover, it gave them access to the Tree of Life, that is, the highest of Worlds. This is confirmed in Genesis 3:22 when YAHVEH-ELOHIM speaks of the man and woman becoming 'like one of Us' if they ate of the Tree of Life and living 'for ever' which, in their state of irresponsibility, could be dangerous for all Existence. Thus Adam and Eve were driven from Eden, down into a fourth World where they were given coats of skins which we, as incarnate souls,

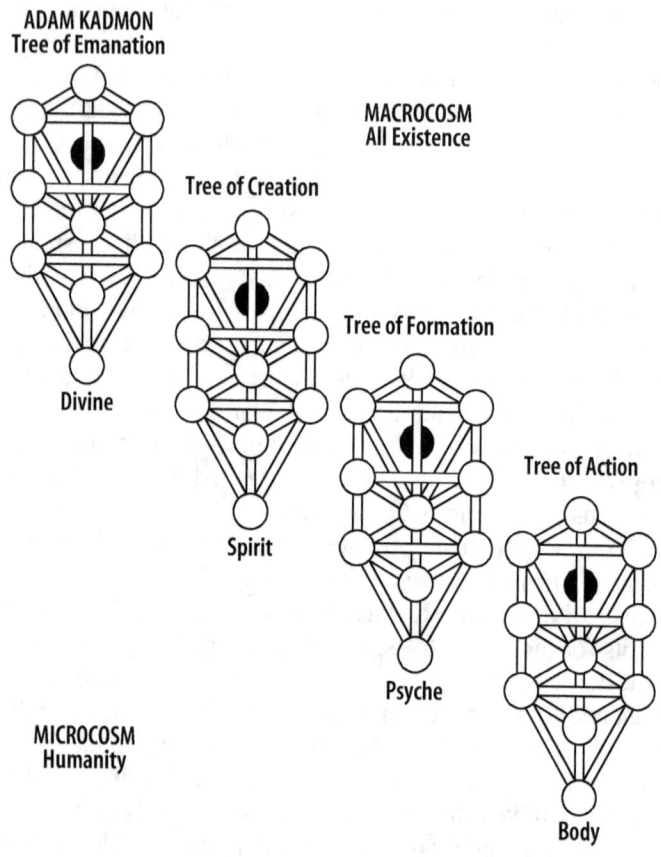

Figure 7—FOUR WORLDS
The totality of Existence is here set out in the form of four universes and the levels within a human being. They are separate but overlapping so as to interact. Thus the lower part of one World relates to the upper section of the Cosmos below. According to Kabbalah, the Bible can be interpreted in a Literal, Allegorical, Metaphysical and Mystical way, according to each level. (Halevi, 20th century).

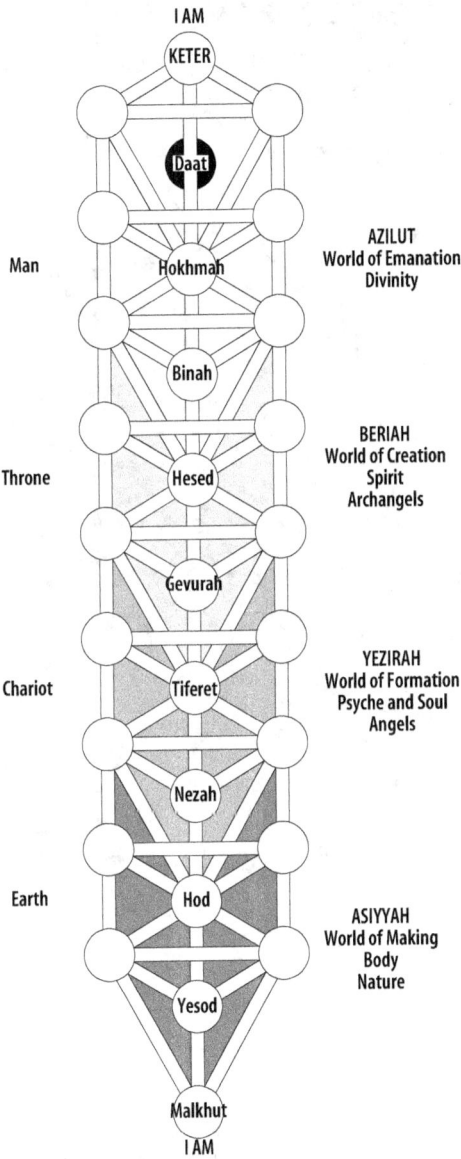

Figure 8—JACOB'S LADDER
The fifth and 'Great Tree' is seen here when the four Worlds are integrated by a vertical line of sefirot on the central column. This is called the Kav *or the Axis Line through which the Divine has access to every level of Existence. The word THAT which hovers between the I AM and I AM above and below is all that exists, between the poles of the two Holy Names. (Halevi, 20th century).*

Figure 9 – EZEKIEL'S VISION
In this old print the four levels are symbolically defined. At the bottom is the realm of the natural World, above this comes the Chariot of Wheels or cosmic cycles. Above is the Throne of Heaven or the realm of the Spirit with the figure of a Fiery Man over all. As Adam Kadmon he represents the Divine image of God. This was seen by the prophet while in a state of mystical contemplation. Symbols as well as diagrams are the language of Kabbalah. The art is to interpret what they mean in the light of experience. (The Bear Bible, 16th century).

wear to this day.* This lowest of realms is called Asiyyah or the World of Action and is represented in Genesis by the four rivers that flow out of Eden, each stream echoing one of the four principles of Emanation, Creation, Formation and Action at the physical level of Existence.

The scriptural basis of the doctrine of the four Worlds is seen not only in Genesis but in Ezekiel's vision (Ezekiel 1) and the verse of the crucial line in Isaiah 43:7—'I have called, created, formed and made him'. This leads on to the fact that a man has these four levels of reality present within him. However before we can set the human scheme out in detail, we must grasp the metaphysics of the Sefirotic Tree which forms the model for all the lower Worlds.

The first World is based upon Ten Divine Attributes plus one unmanifest Attribute. These ten aspects of Adam Kadmon are arranged by Kabbalists according to the Laws generated by the Divine qualities. Overall is the Unity of Divinity as expressed by the symbol of Keter, the Crown. Then there are the two aspects of Hokhmah, Wisdom, and Binah or Understanding, that is, the revealing and reflective side of the Divine mind. These are echoed below in the Divine heart of the Image of God in the Attributes of Hesed or Mercy and Gevurah or Judgement. Just below and at the centre of the Tree is the place of Tiferet or Beauty, sometimes called the Seat of Solomon. Below this, to the left and right, are what are sometimes seen as the Limbs of God that carry out, in active and passive manipulation, the Will of the Divine. These are called by various English translations of the Hebrew words Nezah and Hod, none of which fully describe the functions, but we shall use the terms Eternity and Reverberation respectively. Below, at the place called Yesod or Foundation, is the principle of Generation and reflection of what is below and above. This corresponds to the ordinary ego consciousness in man. And at the very bottom is the sefirah called Malkhut or the Kingdom which is sometimes referred to as the Body of God. Finally, the non-sefirah called Daat or Knowledge is the place where the Will of the Absolute can enter from above to speak or act within this or any other of the lower Worlds that extend as a chain of Trees below the Divine World.

The infrastructure of the Tree is based on several major Laws. The first Law is the Unity of the Whole. The second is the doctrine of the three pillars. These are the middle column of Equilibrium and Grace, the right of Mercy and the left of Severity. As such they keep the

* For a complete account of Creation see the author's *A Kabbalistic Universe* (Kabbalah Society).

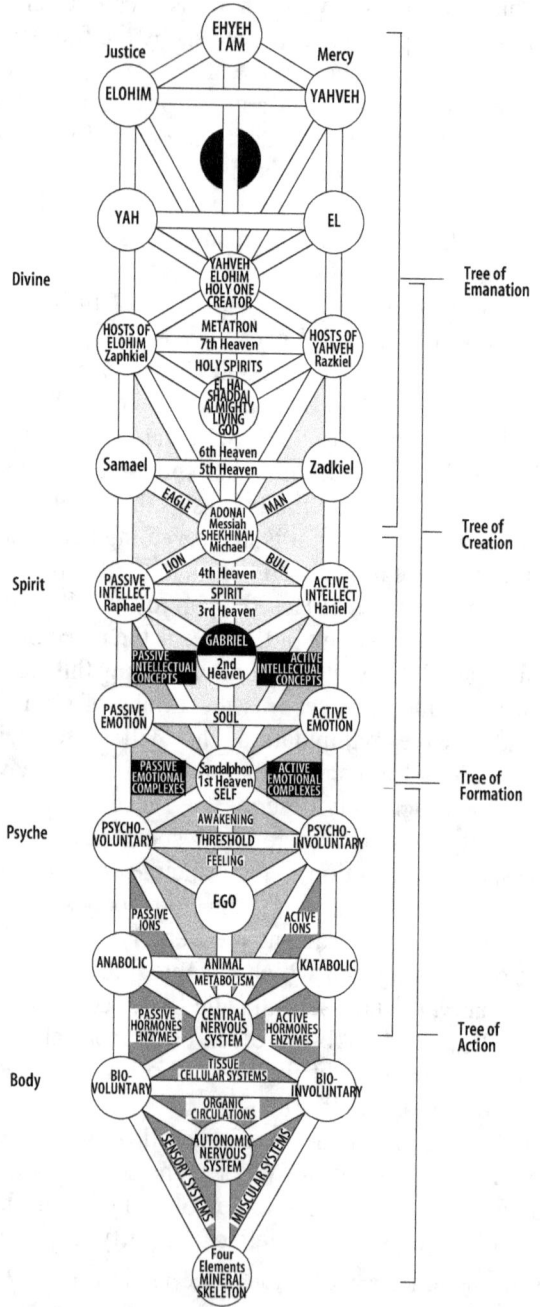

balance of Existence, the two outer ones being active and passive in function with the centre column as the conscious harmoniser. The third Law is the flow of the original sequence of Will as shown by the arrows on the diagram (Figure 5). This describes the unfolding of the ten manifestations through the various active and passive stages under the direction of the central column to resolve into Malkhut, the Kingdom, at the bottom. The fourth Law is that there is a Divine, creative, formative and action level within this prime Tree. The fifth general Law is that of the upper and lower faces, which describe the vertical axis of Mercy and Severity in the Divine scheme. Finally the sixth Law is the division of the various triads which are composed by the sefirot into active and passive functions of the right and left and the triads of consciousness attached to the central column.

The Tree of Emanation gives birth to the Tree of Creation and out of Creation emerges the Tree of Formation which, in turn, gives rise to the Tree of the Natural World. The way each adjacent tree interlocks with its neighbour indicates the interpenetration of this ladder of Worlds. Thus the creative impulse may easily flow down and Providence act efficiently anywhere in Existence. It also allows the possibility of mankind rising up into the higher realms. Tradition says that mankind alone has access to all levels. This is so that Adam may outwardly perceive the Divine reflection in the Cosmic Mirror of Existence. This brings us to the composition of a human being. A man is constructed in the same way as the Image of God. Thus he has four equivalent levels of will, intellect, emotion and action which are expressed in the form of a body, a psyche, a spirit and the Divine spark. These four inward Trees correspond to the four cosmic Trees and as such relate directly to each World and its respective reality.

The physical body, as set out in the bottommost Tree, possesses all the qualities of the World of Action. It is composed of the four elements of solid, liquid, gas and radiation, uses the vegetable processes by which to grow and feed, and the animal principle by which to move about and relate to other creatures. The animal part of man gives him his herd or tribal instincts. This reveals the first division of the human

---

Figure 10 (Left) – GREAT TREE
In this, the general details of the levels are filled in. At the bottom are functions related to human beings within the body and psyche. Above are the spiritual and cosmic dimensions with the Holy Principles at the top which govern all the Worlds through the operation of Providence. In the course of development the Kabbalist learns to enter those higher levels and work with them so as to advance their own and human evolution within the Divine Scheme. (Halevi, 20th century).

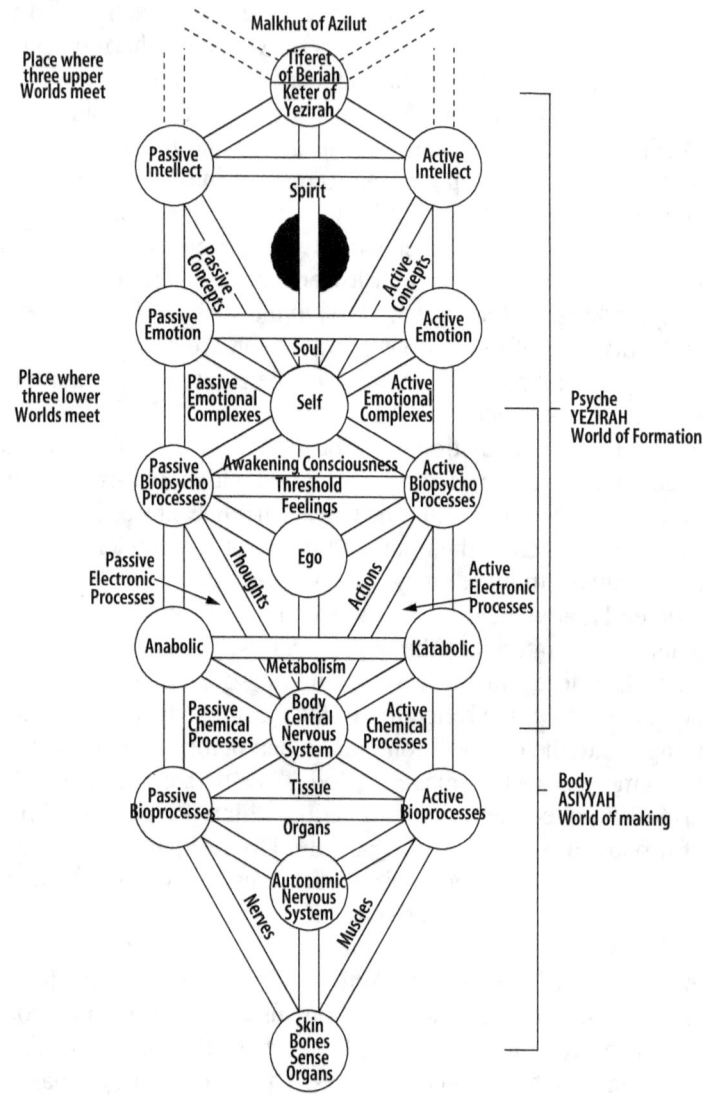

Figure 11 — BODY AND PSYCHE
In order to understand the inner content of the Scripture it is necessary to know the composition and workings of human nature. With this knowledge one is able to discern what different Biblical characters represent. These correspond to certain archetypes. Esau clearly represents the body while Jacob symbolises the soul. Esau's instincts dominated him and so he lost his spiritual inheritance. (Halevi, 20th century).

race: the animal person who wants to dominate and the vegetable person who is content to submit to conditions. The Tree of the body shows the four levels as the mechanical, chemical, electronic and life consciousness levels within the carnal vehicle.

The lower face of the psychological organism fits over the upper face of the physical Tree. Here the natural conscious level of a human being is manifested in the body by the Kingdom or Malkhut of the central nervous system, the two psycho-biological principles, Hod and Nezah, the ego mind, Yesod, and the upper connection of the self, Tiferet. The great lower triad, centred on the ego or ordinary mind, is made up of the sub-triads of thinking, action and feeling which operate as the psychological mechanics of everyday life. The path between the active and passive psycho-biological functions is the threshold of consciousness, beyond which lies the self which is called the Seat of Solomon for the psychological Tree.

Above the self which, it will be observed, has access to the three Worlds of body, psyche and spirit, is the soul. This is the place of self consciousness, conscience and all the deeply emotional events of a person's life. To either side are the active and passive memory banks where emotional experience is stored. Just above these, to the left and right, are the banks of intellectual beliefs arranged on the active or passive side of the psyche. Between them is the great upper triad of the spirit which, as the upper face of the psyche, overlays the lower face of the creative World of Heaven. Here is where the deep unconscious level resides and acts as the dark glass of Knowledge. Above this are the sefirot of Hokhmah and Binah which constitute deep wisdom and understanding at the intellectual level. At the top is Keter, the psychological Crown or the place where the three upper Worlds meet in man. Here the Divine touches the heart of the World of the Spirit and the zenith of the psyche.

Above the psyche are the cosmic realms of Heaven and Divinity. Having set out a general theoretical ground, let us see a brief application of Kabbalistic Principles to Genesis in preparation for the Book of Exodus.

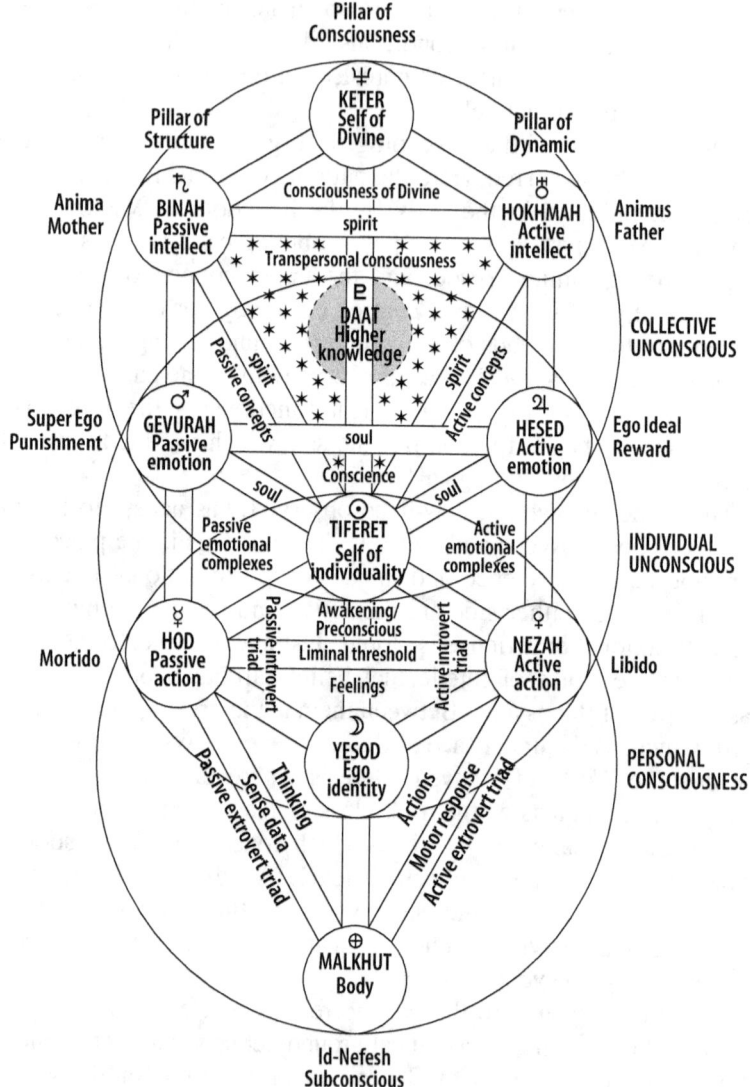

Figure 12 – THE PSYCHE IN DETAIL
While the terms used here are modern, they will enable us to recognise parallels with the Exodus story. As one gets to know the workings of the mind, so there are flashes of inspiration and periods of rebellion. Moving the centre of gravity of consciousness up from the ego to the self is the equivalent to crossing the Red Sea while a moment of enlightenment would be like being with Moses on the summit of Mount Sinai. (Halevi, 20th century).

And the Lord God made
for Adam and his wife
coats of skin
and clothed them
Genesis 3:21

INCARNATION

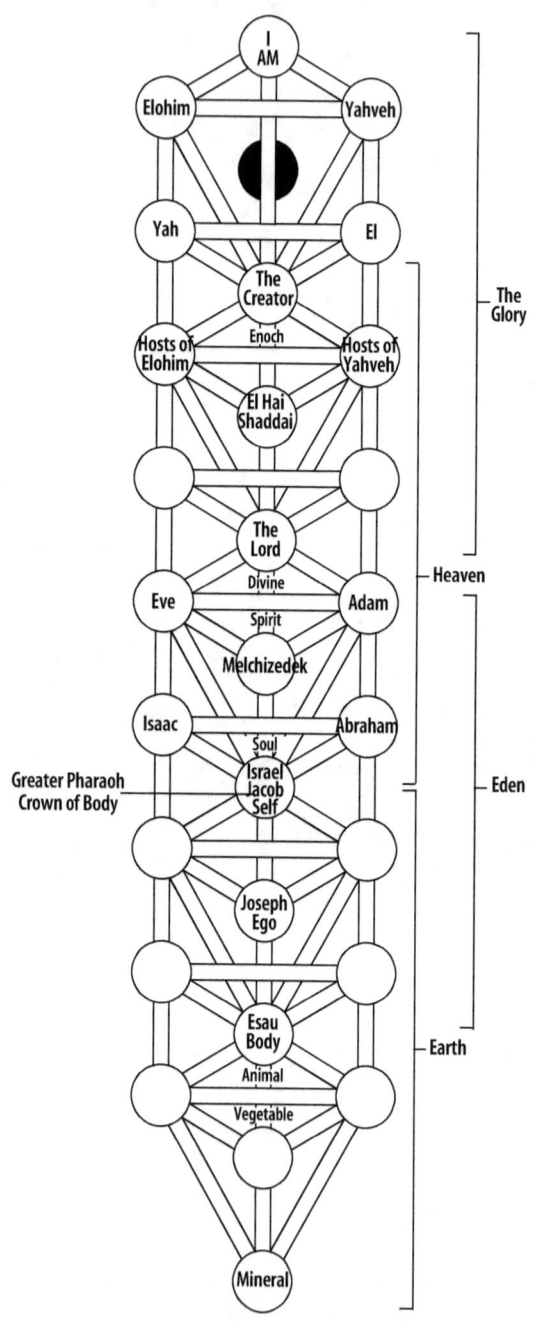

2. *Prologue*
GENESIS

The initial chapters of the Book of Genesis outline the creation of the universe and its inhabitants, including the most complete creature, man. It then describes the forming and division of a Third Adam into man and woman and their fall into matter as they disobey the Will of God. This descent into the lowest of the four Worlds was, oral tradition tells us, foreseen and is part of a great plan in which man, the image of the Divine, descends to the nether levels of existence in order to experience all the Worlds. However, because the gift of free will was still retained by mankind on Earth, the human race disobeyed moral law and offset the flow of evolution to such a degree that the Divine had to consider cancelling the project, despite the fact that an individual like Enoch had managed to attain the highest level the human spirit can reach and walk with God. Fortunately, Noah retained the respect of the Divine and so he was allowed to survive the dramatic removal of a corrupted human race by flood, along with the animal and vegetable kingdoms from the lowest World of Action. A hint of Noah's level of soul comes in legend which says that he did not fall asleep during the whole time that the Ark was afloat upon the waters which are the symbolic element of the World of Formation. When Noah and the preserved creatures with him touched Earth the process of development was begun again in the physical world after the Divine had promised, in the Covenant of the rainbow, never to take such a drastic action against mankind. However, even Noah was not without fault as he became drunk with his own wine and fell into a state of disgrace. This

---
Figure 13 (Left)—BIBLICAL LADDER
Here some of the key Biblical archetypes are placed according to their character. Joseph represents the psychic aspects of the ordinary mind while Jacob is the deeper psychological aspect of the soul. He takes on the name Israel when he reaches the spiritual level of the Self at the place where body, psyche and spirit connect. Isaac and Abraham symbolise polar aspects of the soul with Melchizedek as the principle of mystical experience. Adam and Eve are the archetypes of Father and Mother or male and female aspects of human nature. (Halevi, 20th century).

was a warning that spiritual merit does not place one above the laws of existence but that, on the contrary, more is demanded because one is meant to be an example. His place was taken by his son Shem who carried on the line of spiritual ascent while the rest of humanity became once more preoccupied with earthly power and wealth. This was demonstrated by the building of the Tower of Babel with its aim of entering the upper Worlds by physical means that can never succeed. Shem, tradition tells us, was later to be Jacob's teacher after he had left his father's house.

Abraham is the next major figure to continue the line that represented the spearhead of human spirituality. After he had realised that the beings of the upper Worlds were no more than servants of the Absolute, he was told to leave his country and kin and go to a land which the Lord would show him. This journey to the Holy Country of the Spirit took Abraham through many incidents that tested his faith. Just outside Jerusalem he was initiated by Melchizedek, priest of the Most High God, who transmitted to him the secret knowledge given only to those who have proved themselves receptive and obedient to the Will of God. This brings us to the point where we can begin to place levels and people upon the Ladder of Trees so as to see the Kabbalistic underlay to the story of human destiny and its characters.

If we look at Figure 13 we will see that the topmost Crown has a Divine Name associated with it. This is because this Title expresses, in its full Hebrew of EHYEH ASHER EHYEH or I AM THAT I AM, the Divine intention of God wishing to behold God, that is to unfold down in creation and to return in evolution. The God Names to right and left are those associated with the Merciful and Severe aspects of the Deity, as are those below on the side pillars. The central column carries the Divine Names related to Grace, with the place of God the Creator at the head of the World of Creation, as well as being at the centre of the World of Emanation. Just beneath this position is the seventh Heaven where Enoch, who has been transformed into the Archangel Metatron, resides. Below, at the Foundation and Kingdom of the Divine World, are the God Names of EL HAI SHADDAI and LORD which stand behind the heavenly level of Providence. Adam and Eve occupy the places of Wisdom and Understanding in the Tree of Formation that corresponds to the human psyche. They act as the archetypal father and mother to mankind while, just below in the place of the Spiritual Foundation and psychological Knowledge, is located the figure of Melchizedek, the person, legend says, who has neither father nor

Figure 14—ARK
This boat is an allegorical version of Jacob's Ladder. Its design of many chambers corresponds to the Ladder's many triads with animals representing different kinds of knowledge. These had to be preserved while humanity underwent a terrible purge because they had abused the privilege of free will. When this occurs, in a period like the Dark Ages, monasteries became the Ark that preserve the essence of civilisation. (Rev.T. Bankes's Bible, 19th century).

Figure 15 — MELCHIZEDEK
Here the Righteous King, who had neither father nor mother indicating that he was not of this world, initiates Abram with bread and wine. These are symbols of esoteric theory and practice. Abram is then given the new name of Abraham meaning 'Father of many'. From him came the three monotheistic religions and many schools of the soul and spirit. Melchizedek, alias Enoch, later turns up as Elijah and in other guises to protect evolved individuals. (Rev.T. Bankes's Bible, 19th century).

mother. This is also traditionally the place where the Holy Spirit speaks to an individual as he emerges from the upper psyche and into the World of Creation. Beneath this is the triad of the soul which is manifested in the lives and natures of the three patriarchs.

Abraham holds the right-hand position of Mercy in the triad. Traditionally he is the man who loved God. This Love was tested in the willingness to offer his son Isaac as a sacrifice. According to legend, Abraham was intensely kind and generous. It was these qualities plus his piety, it is said, that drew God down to approach man and so become the God of Earth as well as Heaven. Abraham was called the friend of God and because of this Hesedic relationship God made a covenant with Abraham and promised him not only a son but that he should be the father of many nations, that is, spiritual traditions.

Isaac, Abraham's son, resides on the opposite pillar in the position of Judgement. This place is sometimes called *Pehad* or Fear. This Fear is based upon Divine Justice and its strictness (as against the Merciful pillar), is based upon the fear he experienced while waiting to be sacrificed and his obedience in submitting to the discipline of Abraham his father. As a young man he was very self-controlled, in spite of the hostility of his father's other wife Hagar and his rival brother Ishmael. In later life the excessive strictness of his outlook manifested in the symbol of blindness, which created a conflict between his sons because Judgement without Mercy affects discrimination. Esau, the gruff hunter, was preferred to the gentle shepherd Jacob. Abraham and Isaac balance one another as the merciful and judgemental aspects of the soul.

Jacob, whose name means the 'supplanter', usurped the position of Esau and received both the birthright and blessing of the mystical heritage. As the third patriarch Jacob takes up the central position of the Soul triad on the Psychological Tree. This is because Jacob saw the vision of the Ladder stretching between Heaven and Earth at the place he called Beth El, the House of God (Genesis 28). Seen on the Kabbalistic Ladder that bears his name, this means the place where the physical, psychological and heavenly Trees meet. The two wives of Jacob are said to express the two side columns. Leah the unloved is on the left and Rachel the loved on the right. Perhaps the chief reason for Jacob's central position is his meeting with the Angel at *Peniel* which means the Face of God. Here he rose up from the psychological level of the self which some call 'I' to experience the 'Thou' of the Divine Malkhut or Kingdom in the meeting place of Knowledge. This meeting is the hallmark of the central pillar down which Divinity can manifest directly. The changing of Jacob's name to 'Israel' or 'He who struggled with God' is of esoteric significance as it indicates a transformation of status, a shift of focus from the psychological to the spiritual and so into direct contact with the Divine.

Together, the three patriarchs compose the emotional triad of the Soul. It is here that the Covenant with God is executed by the love of Mercy, the discrimination of Judgement and the truthfulness of Beauty, the self. This triad is the midpoint between the body below and the spirit above. It is the place of conscience, morality, good and evil and the zone wherein a person grows into a living maturing being who can act as a channel to what flows down and what rises up between the terrestrial and celestial Worlds,

Joseph was the first one of the twelve sons of Israel to go down out of Canaan and into Egypt. As Jacob represents the self so Joseph, with his coat of many colours, represents the multi-faceted ego. Dreamer of dreams, Joseph is the screen upon which the psyche exposes itself. Talented, adaptive and intelligent, Joseph is the symbol of the psychological Foundation to the physical crown of the self as expressed by Egypt's greater Pharaoh. This enlightened king of the Natural World honoured Joseph and made use of his psychic gifts. Chosen by Divine Providence to recognise and accept the benefits of a Higher World in his country, he invited Jacob and his family to come down from the spiritual country, given to the patriarchs under the Covenant, into Egypt where they were physically well fed and clothed as any newly born soul and spirit might be.

When Jacob died his remains were returned to the Holy Land to be buried with his fathers. That is, he was taken back up into the World of the Spirit. When Joseph died his body was embalmed and kept in Egypt under the promise that his bones should be taken up from there to Canaan when God would send a deliverer to bring the Israelites up out of Egypt. Thus the first part of the Divine Plan, that man should descend to the lowest World, is symbolised in a family history. The stage is now set for the journey home. In this return the innocent spirit, sent down from the Divine to be incarnated, gains experience in each life, fate and destiny as it evolves back up through the Worlds towards Divinity. As every individual Adam comes to realise that man and the Universe are but reflections of the Divine, he slowly comes to recognise Who is gazing into the Mirror of Existence at Himself. When all the sparks that compose the original Adam Kadmon experience this reality at the End of Time then Divine Face will behold Divine Face.

Figure 16 – JACOB'S DREAM
This is a psychic rather than a mystical vision because Jacob is asleep. By this is meant that he is not awake to what he is experiencing and does not recognise the significance of the beings ascending and descending the Ladder. The word 'angel', a 'messenger', in this case symbolises saints and sages moving between the Worlds through reincarnation. Such advanced souls bring the Teaching to Earth. Many remember previous lives and know why they have been reborn. (Rev.T. Bankes's Bible, 19th century).

Genesis, the Book of Beginnings, ends its description of the descent with the Children of Israel happily sojourning in the Land of Egypt, as yet unsuspecting of what will happen to make them seek their way back to the Promised Land.

3. Bondage of Body
EXODUS 1

The Book of Exodus opens with the names of the twelve sons of Israel who came down into Egypt. That is, the twelve basic types of humanity as expressed in many traditions. These twelve spiritual archetypes came down into Egypt, whose name *Mitzraim* means limitation, bondage, affliction and circumscription in the original Hebrew. The account goes on: 'And all the souls that came out of Jacob's loins were seventy', that is, twelve sons and their children, or the descendants out of the Beriatic World of Spirit, through the Yeziratic World of the psyche and into the physical World of the body or the land of Egypt.

'And they multiplied and waxed exceeding mighty and the Land was filled with them'. This is saying that the creative spirit and the formative soul, in conjunction with the life principle, make the body of a newly born babe grow at great speed as the individual herein symbolised relates to the physical World about him.

Now Exodus speaks of Joseph already being in Egypt. This tells us that the ego or the Foundation of the psyche in the individual is established in the bodily vehicle of the individual to be incarnated as the Daat or Knowledge of Asiyyah, the World of Action. As such it has memories of the psychological World it has come from; in Biblical terms Canaan and its home with its spiritual Father, Israel. This refers to the phenomenon of events before birth sometimes recalled by the very young or spiritually developed. A rabbinic text states: 'As soon as Joseph died, the eyes of the Israelites were also closed as well as their hearts'. That is, they lost the contact with the living memory of their past and roots in the upper Worlds. 'And they began to feel the domination of the stranger' or the constriction of the Egyptians who represent the forces of the body.

This theme is developed further by the verse: 'Now there arose a new King over Egypt who had not known Joseph'. This describes the growing domination of the child's bodily demands and animal will. In the Oral Tradition it is noted that only when Levi, the last of the brothers

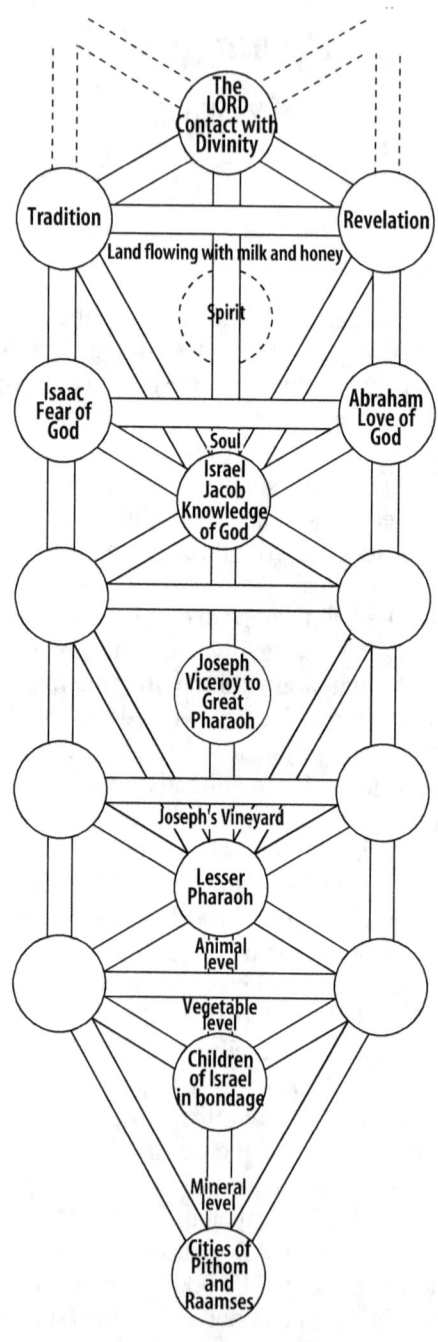

and carrier of the esoteric tradition, was dead that the Egyptians began oppressing the Israelites. This is symbolically seen in the deprivation of the fields and vineyards given by Joseph to his brethren, that is, the interior and independent sustenance of the soul and spirit. In time oppression changed to enslavement as the new Pharaoh, in the manner of the animal soul, slowly forced the Israelites to come under an increasingly psychological, narrow and physically binding regime. For the average individual this is the limiting process of upbringing as education.

When full maturity is reached, as symbolised by the increase from the seventy Israelites to six hundred thousand, a life-time of physical labour is entered upon at the human vegetable level. The various constraints of the physical World, epitomised by the Egyptian task-masters, hold the inner and dulled life of the Children of Israel to the drudgery of building great cities for the glorification of the body or vanity of the ego. Now the names of two of the cities mentioned in the Bible are Pithom, which means 'narrow place', and Raamses which is 'son of the Sun' or the God of the Egyptians. These edifices speak of a materially confined outlook and worship of the Natural World. The Israelites drew no benefits from these enterprises, even on a physical level as, soon after being conscripted, they did not even work for wages but were allowed merely to live so as to labour.

However, a phenomenon of adversity is that it breeds toughness; the more the Israelites were afflicted, the more they increased in strength and number. In order to counteract this tendency, the Pharaoh of the body attempted to kill all the male children born to the Israelites. This move by the animal will was countered, according to Jewish folklore, by two Israelite midwives called Shiphrah, whose name means 'brightness' and Puah, meaning 'splendid', who protected the inner strength being born within the community. This confrontation is the first sign of opposition within the individual between his natural and supernatural aspects. The outer physical resistance of habit and inner psychological social pressure only increase the deep dissatisfaction of the awakening soul. An escape from bondage is sought in many mundane ways, ranging from entertainment to avoid the problem to

Figure 17 (Left)—DESCENT
The going down into Egypt of the Israelites is about the incarnation of the soul. After childhood, when one is looked after, comes adult responsibility. For most people this is a kind of bondage that prevents them from developing their individuality and full potential. In Jewish folklore only the tribe of Levi remembered that they had originally come from the Holy Land of the Spirit. Moses was a Levite. (Halevi, 20th century).

Figure 18—BONDAGE
The Israelites were reduced to poverty at every level. They laboured not for themselves but for the Egyptians. They were just cogs in a repressive state machine. The parallel in life is that people become economic slaves imprisoned by a society which does not allow them to grow. There seems to be no way out of this physical and psychological bondage until something deeper, represented by Moses, emerges. (Rev.T. Bankes's Bible, 19th century).

worldly ambition in order to bury it, but none brings any satisfaction or solution to the sense of being imprisoned. The possibility of escape has to wait for many years until the birth of a particularly powerful focus within the being of the individual or people. This is symbolised by the arising of Moses out of the groaning mass of the psyche of Israel.

4. Birth of Consciousness
EXODUS 2

The parents of Moses, according to legend, were Amram whose name means 'kindred of the High' and Jochebed, meaning 'divine splendour'. Amram was an especially upright man even among the pious tribe of Levi. Because of this he helped to bring the Shekhinah or Divine Presence one stage closer to earth after it had retreated—as the result of Adam's sin and the subsequent sins of his children—to the Seventh Heaven. Amram was the sixth in line after Abraham, Isaac, Jacob, Levi and Kohath to draw the Holy Presence close to mankind again. His wife was no less distinguished in that she was the daughter of Levi and was known for her spiritual quality. However, because of the enslavement, their first child was Miriam, which means 'bitterness', and their second Aaron, which is translated by some rabbis as 'woe unto this pregnancy'. It is also read as 'the mountaineer' and the 'enlightener'.

During the gestation of Moses, Amram and Miriam had dream-visions concerning his future significance to Egypt and Israel. Seen in the individual's progress this is the hint within of inner changes afoot. Such intimations might well occur in dreams that take on a symbolic meaning in that a man might see himself cutting bonds or escaping from prison.

Talmudic legend says that when Moses was born the whole house was filled with a radiance and that he could walk and speak at one day. This describes the emerging within an individual of a centre of consciousness that has a degree of maturity over and above the rest of the being. In order to protect Moses from being killed Jochebed built the child an ark for his preservation and floated it upon the waters to see what Providence would do. Here we see the beginning of trust in relation to matters of the spirit. It is one of the prerequisites in inner work to allow the spirit to lead the life towards its real purpose. As Heaven would have it, Pharaoh's daughter saw him as she bathed in the Nile in order to cleanse herself of leprosy engendered by idol worship.

BIRTH OF CONSCIOUSNESS 49

Thus one of the few Egyptians who valued the inner life saw the child and saved it. There is always one part of the ego which recognises that the Natural World only brings decay and death and perceives something of another, higher World that must be cherished.

This preserving and developing of the Moses principle, whose name means 'drawn from water' or the symbolic element representing the fluidity of the psyche (earth = Asiyyah, water = Yezirah, air = Beriah, fire = Azilut) led to the upbringing and education of Moses in the court of the King of animal men. Thus the awakening consciousness learns the arts and sciences of the Natural World so that it may be acquainted with the ways of mundane life. However, being lifted out of the vegetable slave state into the Animal Kingdom has its dangers. One of the many legends associated with this period of Moses's life describes how, with his remarkable intelligence, he soon excelled his Egyptian teachers. This created, as might be expected, some jealousy from his Egyptian or human animal-level peers. Indeed Balaam the master Magician (later to be sent to curse the Israelites—see Book of Numbers) whom legend places in Pharaoh's court at the time, recognised Moses as a potential danger and warned Pharaoh. Fortunately the archangel Gabriel aided Moses through a life-or-death test, so that his precocious acts were seen as the random luck of a child. Here is the not unknown phenomenon of the supervision of Heaven taking care of the embryo soul in an inherently hostile physical world.

When Moses reached maturity he moved easily as an educated alien in the world of the Egyptians. However, while he was involved in the animal-man's life he was never quite unaware of his own people's suffering—or of the inner life enslaved behind the surface of natural processes. He began to ask questions. One day he saw an Egyptian strike an Israelite and, seeing a basic injustice, killed the Egyptian, we are told in folk-tale, by pronouncing the Name of God. This is to say that he, perceiving the animal aspect of himself assert its will over the psyche, eliminated its dominance by calling upon Divine Grace to kill the inferior desire. The call was immediately answered and so, the rabbis explain, this was not murder but the just death of an evil Egyptian in order to demonstrate to Moses and the Israelites—that is, to the awakening individuality and the rest of the psyche—that the body's dominance could be cast off.

Needless to say, the event soon became known throughout Israel, so that when Moses tried to prevent two Israelites from quarrelling next day he was asked if he intended to kill them. These Israelites, it is recorded, were Dathan and Abiram, two of the most contentious Israelites in the community. They were to oppose him as rebellious aspects of the psyche later in the desert.

Seen kabbalistically, this incident shows that while Grace could aid the rooting out of evil it left much to personal work in dealing with certain perverse aspects of the psyche that resisted spiritual progress. This was quite a different problem from the obvious external enemy of the Egyptian. Confronted by this inner opposition as well as Pharaoh, who now sought his life, Moses fled.

He became, like many of a later generation, a drop-out. He was no longer interested in the ephemeral glamour of Egypt but he did not have the courage to take on Israel's problems. He therefore fled, according to scripture, towards the land of Midian, the place of Striving and Judgement, where—rootless—he could hide away from himself and his destiny.

Sleep and Awakening

5. Initiation: Personal
EXODUS 2

According to legend, Moses did not go straight to the place of Jethro, as recorded in the Bible, but found himself as a fugitive in the camp of the King of Ethiopia. The King of Ethiopia was in the curious position of besieging his own capital because it had been taken by Balaam the magician. As the inner, dark, other self of the psyche Balaam, which means 'master of the people', was an unrighteous soothsayer and sorcerer in that he had developed remarkable psychic powers which he used to influence others without the integrity of the spirit. Seen internally Balaam is that part of the psyche that seeks power without responsibility or reference to anything higher than self-love.

Moses was accepted by the Ethiopians because his radiant face indicated an inner power that they lacked, their physical force being no match for Balaam. However, it was only when the King died that the Ethiopians called upon Moses to lead them against Balaam. Success was accomplished on the first day of Moses's commission and he entered the city to be crowned and given the dead king's widow to wife. This fable illustrates the power of awakened consciousness when applied to problems of a lesser magnitude. However, the allegory does not end there. While he reigned for forty years and increased the power of Ethiopia, he did not cohabit with the queen or worship the nation's gods. The queen eventually turned against him for not consummating their union and the Council of Ethiopia dismissed him but not without honour for services rendered to the country. From this experience in handling a mundane and magical situation, that is on a practical (Asiyyah) and psychological (Yezirah) level, Moses was moved on by Providence to the next stage of his training.

Jethro, whose name means 'excellence' or 'pre-eminence', was a priest of Midian. He was very unusual for his time and place because he did not worship physical idols. He was a God-fearing man and, indeed, has several other names to describe his qualities. Besides the Biblical Hobah and Reuel, which are translated by rabbis as 'beloved son of God' and 'friend of God', he is also called Putiel or 'he hath renounced idolatry'. Because of this he was ostracised by his own people and lived with his seven daughters in the desert. It was at their well that Moses met Zipporah, his future wife, when he defended the girls against hostile shepherds. However, before he married Zipporah he was treated, according to an ancient source, rather badly by Jethro; or so it would seem unless we look deeper, as the legend indicates we should. Jethro was of the same level of development as Balaam for he had been consulted, like the magician, by Pharaoh on the issue of the multiplying Israelites. Legend states that Job, the subject of a later story, was also present at this council. Jethro had advised Pharaoh not to oppress the Hebrews because of their covenant with God. Indeed, he recommended that Pharaoh send them out of Egypt so that they could fulfil their destiny. Pharaoh reacted strongly against this advice and dismissed Jethro. He followed, instead, Balaam's suggestion to drown all the male children.

Before Jethro left Egypt he acquired a remarkable rod. This rod, as Zipporah explained to Moses, had been planted in Jethro's garden where it had rooted into a tree. The origin of the rod is not unfamiliar to many spiritual traditions. It had been created on the eve of the first Sabbath and given to Adam. He had passed it on to Enoch, whose name means 'initiated', who transmitted it to Noah. It had then been given to Shem and passed to Abraham, Isaac and Jacob who, in turn, bequeathed it to Joseph. Jethro had acquired it after Joseph had died and the Egyptians had pillaged Joseph's house.

The rod, tradition tells us, was made of sapphire and weighed forty seals or about ten pounds. Some say it had the Divine Name engraved upon it and others ten letters of various meanings. This rod occurs in later history, in the hands both of Moses and of Aaron, where it is seen sometimes as the Staff of Revelation or the right pillar and sometimes as the Rod of Tradition or the left pillar. Later still, it occurs as King David's sceptre and, when the destruction of the Temple was impending, King Josiah concealed it with the ark until the Messiah should come and claim it. The Christian and Oral Traditions see it as a splinter of the Tree of Knowledge itself and the Moslems regard it with great reverence as the symbol of esoteric knowledge.

Zipporah, after telling Moses of its origins, then explained that her father would accept a man for a son-in-law only if he could pull up the tree. This Moses did with ease but to his surprise Jethro, instead of extending his welcome, threw Moses into a pit where he lived under the most stringent conditions for several years. During this period Zipporah sustained Moses until she got Jethro to go to the pit where he found Moses praying. This convinced Jethro that Moses had a Divine Mission. He released Moses, giving him the sapphire rod.

Seen kabbalistically the above fables, in conjunction with the Bible text, describe how an individual often attempts to move away from his destiny. However, Providence—while not interfering with that person's right to free will—nevertheless provides circumstances whereby the individual is shown his capability. Thus the awakening consciousness, symbolised by Moses, sees how easily his inner power and knowledge make him a King of Ethiopia, that is, a big fish in a small pool. In this situation, however, he rules without any real satisfaction physically, psychologically or spiritually in spite of all outward appearances of success. Eventually the individual must consummate his relationship with these lesser elements of his nature—or be overthrown so that he falls from any Grace he might merit into that twilight zone between Earth and Paradise where only disappointment by the lower and cynicism about the upper Worlds exist to cover a profound failure.

Fortunately Moses recognised that he was not Ethiopian or a worshipper of its gods and freely abdicated the throne. He now knew he was in search of something deeper than physical or psychic phenomena and wandered about the land of striving and judgement until he came to a well. Now a well is a symbol of truth and nourishment and here Moses aided the daughters of a deeply spiritual man to get its waters. Because of this act, he was granted a place in Jethro's house and placed under the most exacting conditions to test whether he was worthy of joining the family or school of Jethro. Here we have a series of severe trials traditionally given to a spiritual candidate in order to judge how serious he is. Jethro, the Friend of God, by giving his daughter in marriage to Moses took him as a disciple.

For a person seeking a spiritual path, this story describes a common experience. A man, by his acts of integrity, comes to the notice of an instructor of souls. In order to test if such actions are genuine, situations are created wherein the prospective student is first invited warmly and then subjected to some difficulties. These usually put off all but the real seeker after truth who, having touched the Sapphire Tree, accepts the trials of initiation to gain entrance to a school of the soul.

Set out on Jacob's Ladder, the story of Moses's flight from Egypt and his marriage to Zipporah traces the ascent of evolving consciousness from the Kingdom or Malkhut of the psyche, which corresponds to the

Tiferet of the body, up to the Ego-Foundation and into the triad composed of Hod-Nezah-Yesod. This is the triangle of Willingness that lies on the frontier between the outer and inner worlds. Here Moses, at the Foundation of the psyche and the Knowledge of the body, resides for several years during his first stage of training. Meanwhile his wife bears him two sons, one of whom is named Gershom which is translated as 'I am in exile in a strange land'. This is the situation of all spiritual aspirants.

6. Moment of Grace
EXODUS 3

When Moses came to Jethro he was in Egyptian clothes; this tells us that, despite his time with the Ethiopians and in the desert, he still used the persona of his upbringing; that is, his ego (which corresponds with Knowledge of the body and the Foundation of the psyche) was so overlaid with the culture and habits he had acquired during his time at Pharaoh's court that he was initially taken as a natural but sophisticated man. However, because he proved to be of a supernatural order, he was accepted for esoteric instruction under Jethro who required Moses not to leave without his consent. The marriage was part of the rule of commitment to an esoteric teacher. Moses was then given his first task of watching over the very young flocks of Jethro's sheep; later he was to watch over the older and then the most mature flocks, seeing both to their nourishment and protection. Now a shepherd in Biblical literature is an allegory for a teacher or instructor and Talmudic commentary draws this idea out in saying that God wished to train Moses in the desert so as to lead the Children of Israel through this same region. During these years with Jethro, Moses learnt much about the terrain and the vegetable and animal kingdoms. In analogue, he studied the action of the elemental world within and without himself and the problems and solutions of both his own vegetable and animal nature, together with acquiring the skills in ordering a group of creatures that were easily panicked and could never see beyond their noses. There are several stories of Moses's strictness and compassion, his discipline in a tight corner and his ability to choose the right places for his charges to rest and feed. Over the forty years he is reported to have been under Jethro's tutelage, Moses lost not a sheep and indeed increased and improved the flock—thus proving himself to Jethro and to God.

By the time Moses was ready for the next stage of his development the Lord, the scriptures state, noted that Israel had reached its limit of suffering under a new Pharaoh. It was then that they recalled the covenant between God and their forefathers and cried out for

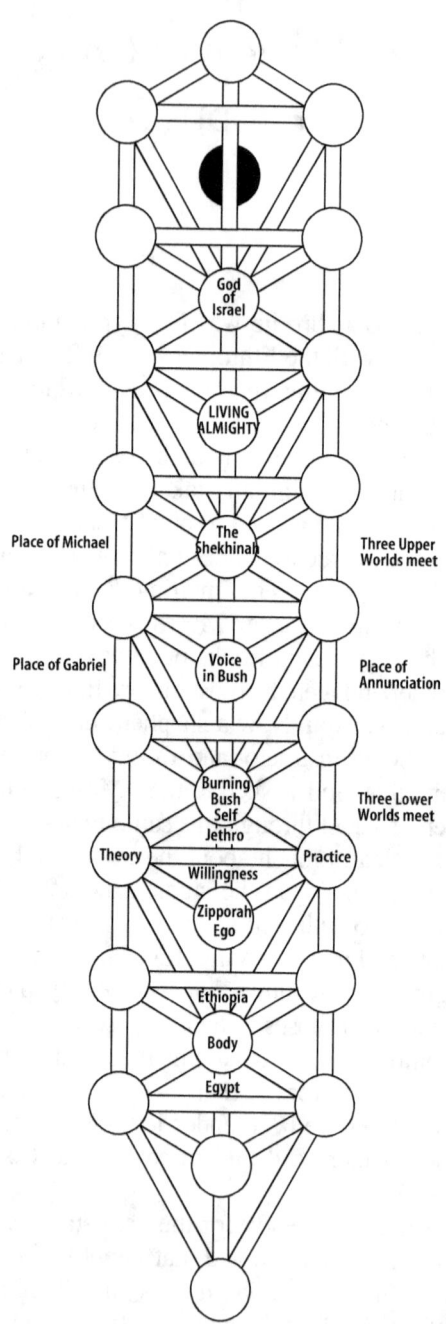

deliverance. That is, the psyche in slavery to the body called up to the Spiritual and Divine Worlds for help. This call was heard.

Exodus 3:1 says: 'Now Moses kept the flock of Jethro his father-in law, the priest of Midian; and he led the flock to the flank of the desert and came to the *(Har Ha ELOHIM)* Mountain of the Divine, even to Horeb'. Horeb means solitude, desolation and many other translations associated with a state of being just prior to a mystical experience. There, *Vayarah Malach YAHVEH aluv*: 'the angel of YAHVEH appeared to him in a flame of fire out of the midst of a thorn bush'. Traditionally this angel (or archangel to be precise) is Michael who, the rabbinical commentary tells us, descended from the place of the Shekhinah or Divine Presence to manifest the Spirit of the Divinity below. Kabbalistically this is Grace as it comes down from the place where three upper Worlds meet to the place where three lower Worlds meet at the self in the centre of the psyche. Here Moses perceived, while none with him could, the Burning Bush that did not consume itself. That is, it was re-created as it burnt; the spiritual level, that of Creation, is the meeting ground between God and man.

When Moses turned aside to see this miraculous event, ELOHIM called to him by name from the midst of the thorn bush (which is considered by the rabbis as the lowest form of that kind of vegetable life, indicating that the Divine Presence is in everything). The use of Moses's name is crucial because it speaks of a high level of individuality which must be reached in order to be able to experience revelation. Moses replied: 'Here am I'. That is, he was fully present. This fact is very important because many a person experiencing such a moment sinks, in panic, into a lesser state of consciousness or even unconsciousness. God then instructed Moses not to come too close but to take off his shoes because he is on *Adamat Kodesh*, Holy Ground. The Hebrew word *Kodesh* also means 'that which is separated and special'. In other words, the place was not of ordinary Earth. It was the highest level of physical experience. This corresponds to the Keter or Crown of the Physical Tree that meets the Tiferet of the psyche and the Malkhut or Kingdom of the Spirit in the self. Here God says that: 'I AM

Figure 19 (Left)—LADDER OF MOSES
Saved by Providence to be brought up at the Egyptian court, Moses learnt the art of leadership. However, he did not forget his Hebrew roots. One day, on seeing an Egyptian abusing an Israelite, he killed the overseer and fled, according to legend, to Ethiopia where as a hero he was tempted by power. Resisting the chance to aggrandise himself, he went on to meet a priestly chieftain Jethro who taught him the skills of living in the wilderness. This was the final part of his training. (Halevi, 20th century).

the God of thy father (Amram), the God of Abraham, the God of Isaac and the God of Jacob'. That is, Yesod, Hesed, Gevurah and Tiferet or the ego that has retained its memory of the Divine and the Soul triad. At this introduction to Divinity Moses hid his face *Ki yaray mahabeet el HaELOHIM*, 'for he feared to look up into the Divine'.

The Oral Tradition inserts, between this moment of coming into the Divine Presence and God speaking about the plight of the Children of Israel, an account of Moses's ascent into the upper Worlds where he is shown the Divine scheme of things. While this material comes down to us in apocryphal fragments written in Greek or Aramaic in the first century of the Common Era, its substance is possibly much older. In it Metatron, alias the translated Enoch, the Angel of the Presence at the Crown of Creation, takes Moses up into Beriah, the World of pure Spirit, accompanied by thousands of celestial beings to the left and right of them for protection against the vast cosmic forces that work in Creation. For the trip Moses is temporarily transformed into a fiery state so that he can move freely at the same level as Metatron through the higher worlds. The conversion of his flesh into fire also indicates a state of illumination.

During this ascension, Moses is shown Purgatory and its various degrees of punishment and Paradise and its thrones of reward. He sees the other-worldly beauty of Eden and Heaven and experiences the profound ecstasy which is reserved for those who perform spiritual work. He is shown the unfolding of the Divine plan, the history of Israel, the building, destruction and rise of the Temple and the coming of the Messiah at the End of Days. He is made acquainted with the purpose of his life and how he will continue teaching even after Earthly death.

Such moments of revelation are not unknown to accompany deep interior illuminations. Suddenly, upon coming into the Presence of the Divine in the self, the being of the individual is raised for a period lasting from a few seconds to several days. During this time the consciousness is lifted right out of the mundane to climb to the pinnacle of incarnate human experience at the Crown of the psychological Tree which is simultaneously the Tiferet of the Spiritual Tree of Creation and the Malkhut of Azilut, the Divine World of Emanation. Here the person glimpses into Creation and sees its workings throughout the lower Worlds. There are many accounts of this kind of experience in Jewish, Christian and Muslim literature. Both the Revelation of St. John and Mohammad's *Night Journey into a Heaven* describe such inner excursions. Time and space change dimension and the phenomenon of the physical World fades in comparison to the richness and power of the upper Worlds as the vision extends in all directions, including the remote past and the distant future. It is often likened to standing on a high mountain and seeing, in an overview, all the events beneath that have happened and will happen. It was upon this Holy mountain that Moses stood and heard God's voice speak of the Children of Israel in bondage below in Egypt.

7. Moment of Decision
EXODUS 3-4

So far we have seen the processes of incarnation, early life, the dissatisfaction with natural pleasures and pains and the attempt to escape into limbo followed by contact with a spiritual mentor. This has led an individual to an arduous training which has earned the merit of being able to reach a place and time wherein Grace descends to give a deep glimpse of a cosmic view of reality. Such a moment of illumination cannot be easily forgotten or ignored. Nevertheless, because free will has been granted to mankind, a human being can accept or reject his or her destiny.

'And Moses hid his face; for he feared to look up unto God'. Now God spoke, saying that the cries of the Israelites had been heard and how the Divine had come down to deliver them and bring them up and out of Egypt into a land flowing with milk and honey. Seen internally, this passage is saying how the individual is to order and transform his body and psyche so as to permanently experience the Spirit. Viewed externally, Moses is about to be given the highly responsible task of bringing a group of souls from a low state of being into the highest most people can reach in one life-time. The role he has been cast for is spelled out in the verse, 'Come now therefore and I will send thee unto Pharaoh that thou mayest bring forth my people'. In this the task is offered, not forced, because it must be an act of free will. In response the stunned Moses backs away. '*Me anochi?*' 'Who am I, that I should go unto Pharaoh and that I should bring out the Children of Israel from Egypt?' Moses cannot believe that it is he who has been selected; that the Divine is addressing him, that his level of development is sufficient even to be considered for the task. The reply is (in the original Hebrew) '*Kee EHYEH imchah*', 'Because I AM with you'. There follows a debate between God and Moses on why he should and should not go.

This debate is important because it sets out very clearly Divine certainty and human doubt. Each time God puts forward a reason to accept, Moses opposes it. God argues gently but firmly, never

Figure 20—DESTINY
In the encounter with the Burning Bush, Moses was told what his mission was. His fate, up to that time, seemed quite random. Now everything came into focus. The miraculous conversion of his staff into a snake indicated, without question, that the Almighty supported him in his destiny. In life a remarkable event sometimes shows the doubter that they are on the right track. The choice to follow that path is, however, still theirs. (Rev.T. Bankes's Bible, 19th century).

demanding that Moses acquiesce in the face of Divine might, because their relationship is one of Love as well as Fear; that is, Moses, being at the place of the Self, is poised between the two outer columns on the central axis of Knowledge. This is confirmed when Moses asks what DIVINE Name he should use. At first the God Name for the highest sefirah of all on Jacob's Ladder is used. This is EHYEH-ASHER-EHYEH or 'I AM THAT I AM' which defines the Will of the Absolute in the Manifested Universe. A few lines later the God-Name YAHVEH is used as a more personal and merciful title for the Children of Israel. This was to become the Name by which God is remembered for all time. In individual terms, here is the Divine making intimate contact with a human being. By this name the person may call upon the Absolute and bring all those parts of his psyche, represented by the Children of Israel, into correct relationship with the Divine.

As God explains to a bewildered Moses the task before both of them, we are shown the possibility of conscious co-operation between God and man. Moses has the scenario of the Exodus set out before him because all except the details are already ordained. Thus the resistance of Pharaoh is anticipated as are the plagues and the departure from Egypt with the Israelites loaded down with gifts from the Egyptian population. The reason for this planning is cosmic, in that the historic context of the event will demonstrate to many unborn generations the power of the Divine Will if God chooses to intervene in the affairs of mankind. It was for this purpose that Israel was selected to be given the law and live out a national destiny. The same principle applies on the individual level in that a spiritual person's life is often subject to both good and bad fortune, in order to show others how to respond to fate according to inner values, because such people are always watched with great interest to see if they live up to their principles. This explains why many saintly individuals have suffered so much in conditions they apparently did not deserve and why they fall harder when they disobey the rules.

To help convince Moses and convert the Israelite disbelief in his authority, the Divine demonstrated the miracles of changing Moses's rod into a serpent and turning the hand of Moses leprous. Kabbalistically this is Divine Will applying Creative principles to overrule the laws of the Worlds of Form and Matter. However, while Moses was deeply impressed, he still resisted the task set, saying he was not eloquent. This problem was solved by the bringing into the situation of Aaron who, as Moses's brother, would complement his work. Here we begin to see how Moses takes up his traditional kabbalistic position on the Nezah of the psychological Tree with Aaron at the Hod. These are the roles of Prophecy and Priesthood manifesting at the level of ordinary man.

Moses eventually accepted the mission but his rôle as the instrument of God's Will was not taken with enthusiasm. This reluctance to perform one's destiny is very familiar to many who have reached this spiritual point. Life up to this moment is very interesting. One studies the theory of esoteric Teaching and performs its practices. Everything is going well in a slow growth process that can be accommodated. Certainly there are occasional crises but these are usually surmounted with help from one's instructor. Suddenly the instructor cannot help any more. We are faced with the I-and-Thou confrontation and the recognition of our purpose in existing. Such a moment happened to Moses at the Burning Bush and he reluctantly turned his face toward the lower Worlds where his work awaited him. For the individual at this point, such a state is familiar because no one, we are told, ever believes he is ready when called to take up his destiny.

8. Moment of Hesitation
EXODUS 4

Before Moses returned to Egypt, he went to Jethro and formally asked to be released from his contract. This is the normal procedure when a disciple leaves his master. Tradition states that Jethro said, 'Go in peace, enter Egypt in peace and leave the land in peace', for he knew that Moses's task was to help redeem those in slavery and bring them to the Holy Mountain. The Oral tradition adds that Moses left for Egypt on the same ass that had carried Abraham to Mount Moriah, which means, according to some, 'the vision of YAHVEH'. This same ass, while being the most ignorant of animals would, according to tradition, know of the Messiah's presence before Israel and bear Him at the End of Days into Jerusalem.

On the way down into Egypt a most curious incident occurred which is recorded in Exodus 4:24-27. In this Moses, who has the *Et matay Ha ELOHIM*, the staff of the ELOHIM in his hand, rests at a lodging place. Here the scripture says that YAHVEH met and sought to kill Moses. Now this incident has puzzled many people over the centuries. Why should God seek to kill Moses after all the trouble taken over him? The answer is simple if one has witnessed a similar event in life where a man or woman who should know better deliberately neglects to carry out his spiritual commitment. Such people, and it does happen, are demoted after several warnings by Providence from that level of spiritual work. They 'die' to its possibilities by avoiding its responsibilities. In Moses's case, the considerable reluctance to go to Egypt reasserted itself and he stopped overlong at the lodging place as an act of laziness or wilfulness. This created a situation where the Divine confronted him and threatened his spiritual life-line. At this point Moses's wife, by circumcising their son, reminded Moses of the Covenant made with his forefathers concerning their relationship with God and his own commitment in particular. She threw the foreskin at Moses's feet (Exodus 4:25) with the words, 'Surely a bridegroom of blood art thou to me'. This sharp reminder of the inter-connection between the body, soul and spirit had the desired effect and Moses's illness in the legend began to abate. The scripture goes on: *Vayiref Mimenu*, 'And He desisted (or withdrew) from him'. That is, the Lord no longer sought to chastise Moses. According to Jewish folklore, Moses was all but swallowed up by the angels of Judgement and Death until Zipporah freed him.

From this dramatic relapse the narrative switches to Egypt, to Aaron who is informed by God of Moses's coming. And so Aaron goes out into the wilderness to meet his brother. They met *Ba Har ELOHIM*, 'in the mountain of God' (Exodus 4:27). That is, the part of an individual which has been growing even within the routine of ordinary life comes to meet the part of himself that has been evolving under discipline. This occurs in the state of psychological Self-consciousness upon the lower slopes of the inner mountain of God. Here is the zone that lies between the Spirit and the Psyche where the two brothers unite and exchange their experiences of the upper and lower Worlds. After their reunion they descend into Egypt and address themselves to the Elders of the Children of Israel. This means that the mutual knowledge of the inner and outer Worlds is brought into the ego consciousness and shown to the more mature parts of the lower psyche. Here the articulate Aaron of Hod explains all the words of God spoken to Moses while Moses, on the active sefirah of Nezah, demonstrates from the pillar of Prophecy the miraculous signs of the rod, serpent and leprous hand.

Because the people actually saw and sensed the miracles they, or the body-bound psyche they represent, believed that the Lord 'had visited them' or was aware of their afflicted condition and so they prostrated themselves. The physically-based reason, feeling and sense triads that surround the ego mind on the Psychological Tree are easily impressed by the supernatural but this also demonstrates the difference between belief and faith. One may believe without knowing what one has seen which is not the same as faith which requires real knowledge. This is proved later again and again as the Israelites revert to disbelief in their incomprehension of what their journey is about.

At this point the miraculous appears in order to show a sense-grounded psychology that there are other dimensions and hope of help. However, redemption is not as instantaneous as many suddenly converted people would like to believe. While Grace may give a glimpse of other Worlds, it will not transform the being of a person unless there has been a great deal of preparation. In the case of the

Israelites there was little or none: there was only the memory of a promise about a distant Land.

This trace of the Covenant deep within everyone's psyche is beautifully illustrated by the rabbinical story of the signs that Jacob had given to Joseph by which to recognise the Redeemer. This piece of knowledge had been passed on to a niece, Sarah, who was still alive. The Elders consulted her about Moses and she confirmed that these were indeed the signs she had been told about by her father. The next task, however, was not to be so easy because, while the Elders of the lower psyche saw the possibility of redemption, they were too weak to go with Moses and Aaron to confront Pharaoh, Lord of the body.

ACTION

9. First Reaction
EXODUS 5-6

Legend tells us that when Moses and Aaron approached Pharaoh it was on his birthday. Because of this he was surrounded by all the vassal rulers of the world who had come to do him homage. Thus he was very surprised when he heard the two Hebrews had not brought any gifts. Because of this he made them wait upon his pleasure. Now while the Talmud describes Pharaoh's palace as a fortress which none could enter, this was easily accomplished by Moses and Aaron with the help of the Archangel Gabriel. After rejecting the pair, Pharaoh chastised his guards and set up others but the same thing occurred. This time, when Moses raised his staff the two ferocious lions at the court entrance welcomed the brothers and it was recognised that the Hebrews were not ordinary people.

Seen kabbalistically, this is the penetration of the body and lower psyche by the presence of Spiritual Knowledge. All the normal physical and psychological patterns are over-ridden and baffled when presented with a higher reality. This situation is beautifully illustrated in the legend which describes how the court was so overawed by the strange light radiating from the Hebrews' countenances that the Egyptian scribes threw down their books and bowed before a deeper truth.

However, Pharaoh was blind in his sensual vision; for when he was asked to release the Israelites that they might go out into the wilderness to sacrifice to the Lord, he asked, 'What is the Name of your God? What lands does He possess? What is His power? What victories has He won?' This is the ego reducing everything to its own sensual experience. Moses replied that Heaven was God's Throne and the Earth His footstool, His shield the Clouds and Lightning his sword; that God created the Universe and brought forth the spirits and souls and nourished and sustained all Existence. Pharaoh answered that he had no need of God, that he had created himself and he had possession of the Nile which is the source of all life in Egypt. So it is with the body-centred person who cannot accept anything beyond the physical. To such an egocentric individual matter creates brain and brain the mind over which his will rules.

However Pharaoh, being logical according to his literal understanding of everything, set his scribes to comb the archives (that is, of the ordinary mind) to see if the Name of the God of the Hebrews could be found. This action was observed by Moses to be futile in a remark about 'seeking the living among the dead'. Here is a situation often experienced by the spiritually-oriented when confronted by the learned who seek authority in books and in others' experience.

This remark of Moses on the limited intelligence of ego did not help to secure the Hebrews' request; Pharaoh instructed his officers to increase the workload of the Israelites and even deprive them of the materials for making bricks. The ego's reaction to any threat to its authority, comforts and desires is fiercely to suppress the enslaved psyche. Understandably, the Israelites protested to Moses how even that small freedom they possessed was now reduced.

Moses approached God with the question of why things were now even more difficult (a situation not unknown at the beginning of spiritual work). The answer came back (Exodus 6:1), 'Now shalt thou see what I will do to Pharaoh, for with a strong hand shall he send them away'. That is, the conditions for a dynamic confrontation were being created whereby the body's considerable power would be made to give the psyche its initial push towards the journey of the spirit. In individual development this situation frequently occurs, in that physical laziness and psychological inertia are overcome by the sheer unacceptability of a situation. Something has to be done to get out of a grinding routine or escape from day-dreams of a better life.

At this point of deepest despair of Israel, the Bible speaks again of the Covenant with the three Patriarchs. Here the scripture says that the soul triad composed of Abraham, Isaac and Jacob knows God by the Name EL SHADDAI, that is, the ALMIGHTY GOD, but *not* 'by my Name YAHVEH'. The Divine Name given to Moses on the Holy Mountain establishes a direct connection between the Children of Israel and the Creator. The implication of this is enormous, on the individual level, in that if this special Name is called upon in prayer the Divine will hold direct converse. Out of this intimate contact between the individual and God comes the offer of redemption continually repeated in the Bible. However, the habitual patterns of the psyche make for lethargy and disbelief which is symbolised in the moral collapse of the Israelites at increased Egyptian pressure. A despairing Moses asks God, 'How will Pharaoh grasp that which even the Israelites do not understand ?'

10. Phenomena
EXODUS 6-7

At the end of Exodus chapter 6 is a lineage of the twelve tribes. This reminds us that the going-out of Egypt is based upon a tribal saga which has been adapted for the purpose; for it must be remembered that the priestly scribes were not so concerned with historical fact as with living mythologies, interweaving the inner and outer and upper and lower Worlds which echo episodes in the life of an individual beginning spiritual work.

Exodus 7 begins: 'And the Lord said unto Moses, see I have made thee a god unto Pharaoh; and Aaron thy brother shall be thy prophet. Thou shalt speak unto Pharaoh, that he send the Children of Israel out of his land. And I will harden Pharaoh's heart, and multiply My signs and My wonders in the land of Egypt'. With these awesome lines the Creator of the Universe speaks to a mortal about a plan that has been devised to demonstrate the presence of a power greater than any other known on Earth or indeed in the Heavens. Israel's redemption by a series of miraculous events would mark the birth of a nation selected to show Divine Will at work, be it reward, punishment or Grace-given freedom. So it is with an individual at this stage of development. At this point dramatic internal and external events shake and change the pattern and course of his life.

When Moses and Aaron again came before Pharaoh to ask for the release of the Israelites they performed the miracle of turning the rod into a serpent. Jewish folklore says that the magician Balaam was present at court and passed the opinion that Moses and Aaron were magicians. Pharaoh then ordered the Egyptian priests to duplicate the performance with their rods, which they did. The Hebrew serpent, however, swallowed up the Egyptian snakes; Pharaoh was displeased but Balaam devalued the event by saying that it was the nature of snakes to devour each other.

The above tells us that the Divine can be opposed by occult power, that is, human will manipulating the psychological World of Formation.

Figure 21 — KNOWLEDGE
The contest between Moses and Pharaoh's magicians is about different orders of knowledge. Magic, of which the Egyptians were masters, belongs to the psychic realm of Formation. This means that they could produce and manipulate images. Moses, in contrast, had access to spiritual power which can actually transform situations because it is creative and cosmic in scale. This difference is symbolised by the Egyptian serpents being consumed by Moses' staff-snake of Higher Knowledge. (Rev.T. Bankes's Bible, 19th century).

Thus a master such as Balaam or indeed anyone well trained in a school of magic would know how to operate in that realm so as to make and dissolve forms at will. The Egyptian adepts could harness the subtle part of the upper physical world to their will and play upon the senses as well as influence the psychological level of the viewer so that he perceived a form standing before him. Moses and Aaron, by contrast, were under obedience to the Will of God. They were agents for the miraculous. The word miracle is crucial: in the Hebrew it is *Mofat* which is translated by the rabbis as 'wonder'. This does not belong to the World of Yeziratic forms but to Creation which is cosmic and thus is of quite a different order. This is shown in the swallowing-up of the Egyptian snakes by the Divine serpent.

Balaam cannot see beyond his own vanity and explains the episode away, more to justify himself than to excuse the Egyptian failure. Pharaoh, however, was now deeply impressed, the fable records, especially when he observed that Aaron's rod, in assuming its original form, showed no sign of bulging with its intake of the other rods. Clearly the Hebrew's power was greater. However, he says, 'Had you asked for only a few thousand people to go I would have agreed but for all, no'. While conceding a little out of superstitious fear, he could not let his dominion be threatened.

The significance of the confrontation between magic and miracles in the evolution of the individual is that, about this period of development, there is usually an encounter with such phenomena. At first the untrained eye cannot tell the difference because both classes are seen as supernatural. Thus many initially mistake the occult powers of people who have cultivated such skills as being signs of spiritual development. There are spiritual magi but they are rare because magic is, more often than not, the pursuit of strange powers rather than service to the Divine. The hallmark of the miracle is that it does not originate from a human being. It may come down through a person but he is merely the conduit of Creative action. However, such human instruments usually have a high degree of purity or the descending spirit will not flow through their being. The cardinal quality of the miracle is the cosmic dimension and its place in a grand design. Miracles are usually performed in order to demonstrate some universal principle or to clear the way for some great event that will affect the spiritual life of that person (or many people) for all time. The episode of the ten plagues is such a case.

11. *Physical Resistance*
EXODUS 8-9

According to rabbinical tradition the ten plagues were divided into four stages. Three of the plagues were implemented by Aaron, three by Moses, one by the two together and the last three by direct Divine intervention. Seen Kabbalistically, these may be viewed as the four Worlds, the left and right pillars, the central pillar and the supernal triad at the top of the Tree of the Ten Plagues. Moreover, the rabbis see Aaron's plagues as to do with earth and water while Moses's are seen as involved with air and fire. This interpretation is again a view of the Four Levels of Existence.

The first plague, of the river turned to blood, was inflicted directly after the third time that Pharaoh had been requested to let the Israelites go. This describes another esoteric phenomenon: when Providence is about to do something, it first hints, then indicates strongly before the final act of what is to happen comes to pass. So it was with Pharaoh that after the third opportunity had been ignored the plagues began.

For a whole week the Egyptians witnessed the presence of death through an excess of blood, the symbol of life. The Nile, the main artery of their life, stank with dead fish and all the waters were polluted throughout the land. The meaning of this is that the vitality of the physical World went into reverse to reveal just how vulnerable the natural kingdom was when an over-balance of life became deadly to itself. Despite this lesson Pharaoh still remained obdurate. Thus it is that even when the body is hurt it will still cling to the psyche and not let it go beyond its physical ruler.

The second plague, of frogs emerging out of the river to infest the land, represents the movement of the action from the lowest elemental sefirah of Malkhut up to Yesod. Here the Yesodic image of the frog afflicts the Egyptians with the unpleasant experience of uncleanness in everything touched. Indeed, so noxious was their presence that Pharaoh said that if the frogs returned to their natural habitat he would let the Israelites go. The request was complied with but Pharaoh reversed his

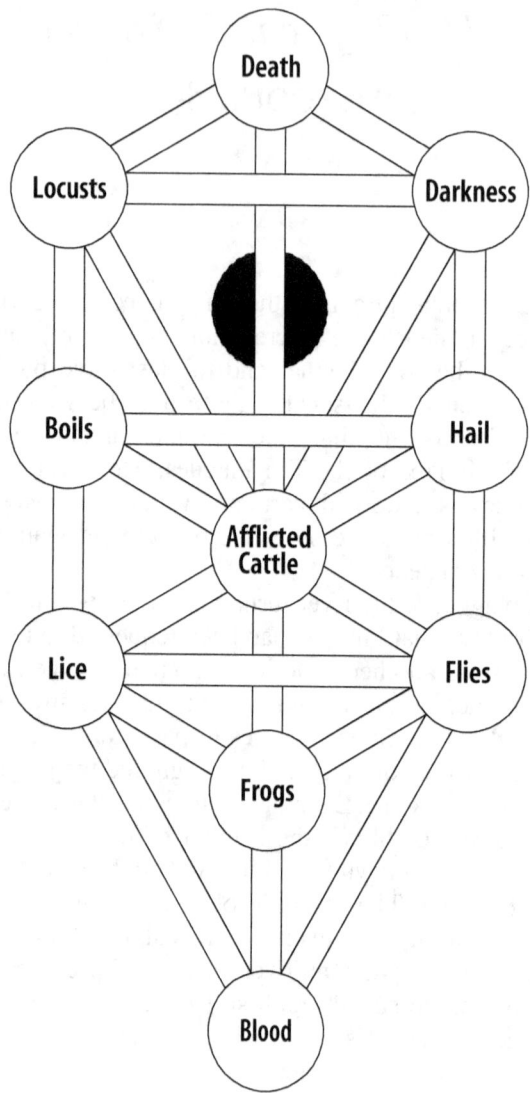

Figure 22 — TEN PLAGUES
These represent a negative aspect of the Sefirot. The Hebrew word 'blood' is related to the Earth and is therefore at the very bottom. Boils and hail symbolise excessive implosion and explosion, while Death is the ultimate affliction. These were punishments of the body which Egypt symbolised. Pharaoh represents the basic instincts which are hard to overcome. The plagues represent physical manifestations of imbalance. (Halevi, 20th century).

Physical Resistance

decision once the duress was gone from the land. This is characteristic of a sense-based decision; when the pressure comes off, the body has a very short memory.

Pharaoh's change of mind was influenced by the fact that the Egyptian magicians could reproduce the first two plagues, as any party conjuror can replicate the appearance of magical phenomena. However, the third plague of lice could not be duplicated and the magicians declared that this was indeed the finger of ELOHIM, the Gods. In spite of this setback, Pharaoh would not let the Israelites go and so all Egypt was smitten with lice that crawled over man and beast. This revolting state at the individual level might be likened to an afflicted Hod or mental processes where the precision of this sefirah is marred in its function, so producing psychosomatic disorders.

When Moses's request was again rejected, the plague of flies, or wild beasts as some translate it, began. This may be seen as an over-active Nezah or prolific swarms of animal life reaching into every part of the organism. The disruption of Egypt's life shocked Pharaoh into action and he asked for Moses to call off the affliction, especially when he observed that the Israelites in the Land of Goshen were in no way affected by the plague. This indicates the beginning of the separation of the body from the psyche and it is confirmed in the verse of Exodus 8:19, 'And I will put a division between My people and thy people'. Pharaoh said, 'Go and sacrifice to your God, but within the frontiers of this country'. The body still held fast to the psyche. The confrontation was intensified when Moses insisted, because he knew the Egyptians would become violent, that the Israelites go right out into the wilderness to perform their ritual. Pharaoh, in desperation, conceded to the condition but said 'only do not go far'. The animal soul still held hard.

In the last verses of Exodus chapter 8 God advises Moses not to allow Pharaoh any room to manoeuvre. This is when the contest moves up to the Tiferet position, the place of Truth, on the Tree of Plagues. Here the will of God is stated plainly to the body to let the psyche be free of slavery in order to worship. If this request is refused, then all the vital functions in the body will come under pressure to make it lose its already failing grip, which is symbolised in the report that no beast of Israel is touched by the terrible plague that fell upon the herds of Egypt. Even so, Pharaoh remains adamant as the animal soul often does in the face of events too large for it to grasp.

The next two plagues, of boils and hail, relate to Gevurah and Hesed and follow the negative aspects of these two sefirot, in that the boils are concentrated form and the hail the uncontrolled force of the respective principles. These two manifestations descend upon the Egyptians with such power that even the magicians who, up till now, could protect themselves, were afflicted by them while the Israelites remained unaffected. Everything within Egypt was beaten, burnt or blasted until the sensual will, represented by Pharaoh, bowed under the onslaught and asked for the plagues to end, promising in desperation to release Israel. This is a familiar situation in time of great stress when the body will promise anything to survive. When the plagues were removed Pharaoh again reverted to his former attitudes, as people often do after a crisis. But this respite was not the end of the matter, for he still would not allow the Children of Israel to go up out of the Land of Constriction.

12. Breakthrough
EXODUS 10-12

Before Moses and Aaron approached Pharaoh for the eighth time the Lord said to them, 'for I have hardened his heart, and the heart of his servants, that I might shew these signs before him, and that thou mayest tell in the ears of thy son and of thy son's son, what things I have wrought in Egypt, and My signs which I have done among them, that ye may know how I am the Lord'. The scale of this passage speaks of the majesty of the Creator of the Universe and the effect on human history of Divine intervention which can override the world of natural laws. On the individual level, the effect of such an intrusion into a routine existence usually profoundly shakes the person out of his habits and opens up questions as to the meaning of life. Anyone on an inner path knows of at least one miracle in his life that has awakened him out of spiritual sleep. On the scale of a nation Israel, at this moment in the Exodus story, is approaching just such a point of awakening.

When Moses and Aaron, who represent the only as-yet developed part of the psyche, stood before Pharaoh the animal soul and repeated the words of the Lord, 'How long wilt thou refuse to humble thyself before Me? Let My people go, that they may serve Me', Pharaoh at first gave ground. He then, on hearing that the demand was still for all the Israelites, reversed his decision and had the brothers driven from his court (or consciousness). This reaction brought its result. The locusts that fell upon Egypt began to devour what wealth and resources had been left after the other plagues. Soon there was nothing green in the land; that is, the basic vegetable soul that supports the animal soul was now threatened. This frightened Pharaoh and he began to beg for help. The animal soul becomes quite irrational when faced with extinction. However, yet again he became self-assured once the locusts had gone and Egypt was no longer threatened. The ninth plague of darkness then descended upon all Egypt except for the Land of Goshen.

Seen Kabbalistically, the locusts represent the destruction of Binah or the life-form system of Egypt while the darkness is the curtailment of Hokhmah or the life force. Thus, during the darkness, no Egyptians stirred for three days. This created a situation of total paralysis for both the vegetable and animal level of Egypt and so Pharaoh was forced to summon Moses and tell him to take the Israelites and go and worship the Lord. However, this was on condition that their flocks must be left behind; that is, the natural wealth or vitality of the Israelites was to be retained by Egypt. Moses said that Israel needed the flocks for food and for sacrifice but Pharaoh reacted as only the panic-stricken animal soul can, by dismissing the whole business from his uncomprehending mind and threatening death if he should ever see Moses again. Moses responded gravely saying, 'Indeed I shall never see your face again'.

In preparation for the separation of the two nations or levels, the Divine now instructed Moses to get the Israelites ready. They were to approach the Egyptians and ask them for jewellery and gold, that is for the riches of the physical world. Then they were to prepare for the Passover which was a ritual especially designed to draw all the people, or the different aspects of the psyche, together into a co-ordinated whole and so make this momentous time into a profound initiation. The individual parallel is often the same, in that some ritual act is performed to mark a change of state. In some traditions there are elaborate ceremonies, in others a simple but potent gesture is made to indicate the passage from bondage to freedom.

The form of the Passover ritual is described in detail in the Bible. In the beginning it is seen as taking place in the first month of the year and on the tenth day, that is, at the beginning of a new cycle and after the first ten stages of sefirotic preparation are completed. On this day a lamb without blemish is taken into the household and kept by the community until the fourteenth day, that is half a Yesodic or Lunar cycle, when it is slaughtered at the crucial point of dusk in the daily rhythm. Now, while these instructions may seem primitive to us they were within the context of a time which accepted esoteric ideas in the ritual form of local custom. Thus the lamb is the killing of the animal will in Israel and its blood smeared on the door lintel the outward sign of the achievement. It was also a protection against the Angel of Death who was to pass over the Land, taking the lives of Egyptian first-born and afflicting the gods of Egypt.

The detailed account of what is to be eaten at this last supper in Egypt is full of symbolism which is used up to the present time in every Jewish household that celebrates the Passover. There is, for example, the dish that looks like cement. This, with salt water and bitter herbs,

Figure 23—ANGEL OF DEATH
Here the firstborn of Egypt are struck down. This physical shock enables the soul, represented by the Israelites, to escape the domination of the body. Sometimes a grave illness makes an individual contemplate their mortality and begin a new kind of life based on spiritual principles. Seen another way, some things have to die before starting on the Path to the Promised Land. (Rev.T. Bankes's Bible, 19th century).

represents the hard labour, tears and harshness of that period. It is a custom that the menfolk lean on cushions to recall the ease of the Egyptians and many other symbols, such as unleavened bread and the awaited angel's wine cup, act as reminders of this historic and personal stage of development.

Perhaps the most esoteric instruction is the method by which one eats this last supper. The text runs, 'You shall have your loins girded, your shoes on your feet and your staff in your hand and ye shall eat it in haste'. Today the national urgency has gone from the Passover but the spiritual implication is made plain in the ceremony where each person must consider as if he were actually an Israelite in readiness to leave the Land of Bondage.

The Israelites were told to be prepared for rapid departure because the most devastating plague was about to strike Egypt. The death of the first-born was to sever the connection between the body and the psyche. In the shock the Egyptians would be so preoccupied that they would allow the Israelites to go. On the individual level a shock often releases the psyche from its body-bound habits and precipitates inner movement. Thus when the Angel of Death had destroyed the first-born, the link with Egypt was broken and the Israelites could go, taking everything they possessed with them.

As the Israelites left the House of Bondage the Egyptians gave them everything they wanted and more in order to be rid of them before all Egypt was destroyed. On the individual level this initial freedom is only the beginning for, while the body had been subdued into submission, the psyche, like the Children of Israel at this point, is still a tribal rabble or unorganised collection of feelings, thoughts and actions. The ordering of such undisciplined elements is not instantaneous nor is the determination of the animal soul so easily ignored after the shock of its defeat has passed.

13. Start of Journey
EXODUS 13-14

In order to give a deep sense of initiation, a set of ordinances was given to the Israelites to be carried out on the Night of the Passover for ever. Such practices are not uncommon in the early stage of a spiritual path. Taking the vegetable level of activity, the preoccupation with food, the Passover meal was transformed into a ritual that raised the level of whoever took part. This annual remembrance of the Exodus was to be particularly recalled by the first-born of the household, not only because they were passed over by the Angel of Death but also because this status represents the beginning of a new generation, a new life. Likewise the practice of eating unleavened bread for seven days was to remind everyone of the seven stages of ascent out of slavery; that is, mastery of the body and the ego, attainment of willingness, then will, the submission of the soul, access to the spirit and contact with the Divine. Alas, these steps have been overlaid in the Passover liturgy.

The Children of Israel took the bones of Joseph with them as he had requested, so that he might be buried with his forefathers in the Promised Land. This is the symbolic withdrawal of the first Hebrew to come down to sojourn in Egypt. With the removal of the bones the process of descent into the flesh is over and the reascent begins. In Hebrew this return is called *Teshuvah* which is paralleled in the individual as the beginning of redemption.

Before the events described in the scriptures, Jewish folklore records an earlier attempt to reach the Promised Land which, from the individual point of view, is instructive. Tradition tells us that there appeared, in the tribe of Ephraim son of Joseph, a man who said that God had told him to lead the Israelites out of Egypt. Now, being of aristocratic descent because of Joseph's position and influence in Egypt, the Ephraimites assumed that the rest of the tribes would follow. But this was not to be, for the time was not right and neither was this the man, although he believed he was inspired by a vision. Nevertheless his own tribe followed him into the desert bearing only weapons and money for they expected to purchase, or take by force, provisions on the way. When they became hungry they approached some shepherds for food who, of course, had no use for money in the desert and so the Ephraimites attacked them. This brought a violent response from the local inhabitants who massacred all the Ephraimites bar ten who returned to Egypt to tell the story. The message for the Kabbalist is plain. One cannot attempt the inner journey without real preparation. Force and worldly wealth are useless in the spiritual dimension and visions do not always originate from a Divine Source. They can be generated by a man's own vanity and pride of an inheritance which is not earned. The lesson is that the shortest route is not always the best. This failure occurs in individual cases where unprepared people who have attempted a quick or direct route through drugs or excessive practices have damaged their bodies or crippled their psyches.

For this reason Moses took a detour away from the shortest route to avoid the Israelites being frightened by the still-unburied bodies of the first excursion into the psychological desert between the physical Kingdom of Egypt and the spiritual Land of Canaan. The stark hint of forthcoming strife might also deter a people that still thought, felt and acted like slaves. After 430 years of servility the Israelites had all but lost their sense of dignity; moreover, with the growth of the tribes into a great multitude the sense of family had been undermined by competition, division, rivalry and disunion. Seen on the personal level, the psyche is simple in the young but, with maturity, life becomes more complex as the person's nature becomes manifold and at odds with itself, as different emotional needs and intellectual concepts strive one against the other in various levels of the psyche. This creates the characteristic contradictions and disarray within the conscious and unconscious aspects of the average untrained person. It was in this state that the Israelites encamped on the edge of the wilderness at Etham, which means 'the border of the Sea'.

In Kabbalistic terms, the Red Sea is the edge of the Yeziratic World or the frontier of the unconscious, stretched between the Hod and Nezah of the psychological Tree. There, the scriptures say, the Lord went before them with a pillar of cloud by day and a pillar of fire by night. This symbol of Divine Guidance was to lead them through the years in the desert. Individuals who reach this stage recognise this presence in their lives, both in moments of illumination and in psychological darkness. The central pillar is the Shekhinah, or Divine Presence, which is perceptible to those in spiritual work.

START OF JOURNEY

While the Israelites camped by the sea, Egypt recovered from its shock; and Pharaoh, his heart hardened in revenge, now considered how he might strike the Israelites as they lay entrapped between the Wilderness and the Sea. On the personal level this can be seen as the body's response to the psyche taking the initiative. Such destructive action by the animal soul is not unknown. Passion has its dark side and a powerful death-wish if its desire is thwarted.

In this state of malevolence Pharaoh and his hosts rode out into the Wilderness to destroy the Israelites. At the sight of the approaching army many Israelites panicked and said to Moses, 'Were there no graves in Egypt that you should have brought us here to die in the Wilderness?' This cry is not uncommon when the first crisis after the initial change manifests. The inferior parts of the psyche say, 'Is not this what we said would happen? Let us alone to serve the body. It is better for us to be slaves than die in the Wilderness of the unknown'.

Here begins the long internal struggle between different parts of the psyche, as represented by different factions amongst the tribes. At the first difficulties the most hidebound elements react according to their time-worn grooves. Moses and Aaron, who stand on the right and left pillars respectively at Nezah and Hod, answer them by saying, 'Fear ye not, stand still and see the salvation of the Lord'. That is, become inwardly centred and watch Divinity operate. At this stage it is only hope and belief that can hold the untrained psyche steady when confronted by the concerted armies of the body. 'The Lord shall fight for you and ye shall hold your peace', Moses said as Pharaoh's hosts drew near.

14. Point of No Return
Exodus 14-15

When the Israelites panicked at the sight of the Egyptians they were instructed to strike camp. Moses then lifted the staff that had been created at the beginning of the World and stretched it out over the waters which at first—according to folklore—did not acknowledge his human command. But when the sea perceived that the staff bore the Divine Name, it fled on either side. Tradition tells us that this division occurred on Earth and in all the Worlds above so that Grace might descend directly to aid the Israelites in their escape. In individual experience this is witnessed when everything related to a major internal transformation is reflected in external events which concur with the change in the state of the person. According to another oral tradition, the Red Sea did not part until the first Israelite set his foot in it, believing that it *would* part, and yet another tells us how the tribes contended to be the first to cross. All these anecdotes describe the various attitudes of different parts of the psyche to taking the initial step to the point of no return.

Rabbinical literature informs us that the dividing of the Sea was the first of ten miracles associated with the passage across it. These events include twelve paths that opened up, one for each tribe; sweet water flowing out of brine by which the Israelites satisfied their thirst; and the phenomenon that whatever the Israelites desired, such as an apple, could be plucked from the waves. These and the other strange happenings signified the entrance into a totally different domain. This was an act of Grace allowing a taste of the good things to come. Such phenomena are often experienced by those rising out of the mundane state into a higher condition. In these transitory states, glimpses and tastes of Eden occur and unexpected opportunities present themselves to the individual who, for a honeymoon period, experiences possibilities hitherto only read about in esoteric fairy tales or sacred literature.

Jewish folklore speaks of the confrontation, at this point, between the angel of Egypt, Uzza, and the Archangel Michael, the defender of

Israel. In this contest, which describes not only the celestial conflict but the battle between the lower archetypes of the body and higher archetypes of the psyche, the gods of Egypt are chastised for their ingratitude towards the House of Israel whose wisdom had saved their nation from famine at the time of Joseph. That is, the animal soul had forgotten the presence of the spirit which gave it vision and life; instead it had enslaved Israelite children or the psyche that sojourned within the land of the body.

'And the Angel of God which went before the camp of Israel removed and went behind them; and the pillar of the cloud came between the camp of Israel and the camp of Egypt' (Exodus 14:19). Thus there was no contact as the Egyptians pursued the Israelites through the pathway in the Sea. The text then goes on to say how the Lord looked at the Egyptian host, through the pillar of fire and cloud, and troubled them so that they cried, 'Let us flee from the face of Israel for the Lord fighteth for them'. This describes the turning point in the conflict between the body and the psyche in that the animal soul begins to realise that it cannot perform outside its domain. Thus the Egyptian host starts to falter as it gets further and further from its own shore, that is across the zone that divides the psyche from the body. The folk saga goes on to say that, despite this moving out of their depth, the Egyptians still sought to hurt the Israelites with arrows and spears backed by the frightening blasts of trumpets and horns. These were met by the counter-cracks of thunder and bolts of lightning from the angelic hosts. In the individual context these symbolise the activities of the deep unconscious or higher psychological centres that operate above the ego as it separates out from being the slave, or Daat of Knowledge, of the body to become the honourable servant of the psyche.

When all the Israelites had reached the far side of the Red Sea, Moses was instructed to stretch out his hand so that the sea might return to its proper place. So it was that the Egyptians, who could pursue as long as there was dry land, were caught between two Worlds as the waters poured back. Such a situation is not unknown among those who pursue an interest in power into the dangerous waters of sorcery and magic. Here, drowning in treacherous tides is a risk for those whose feet leave the ground but who have no wish to reach the far shore.

Legend has it that when the Egyptians were drowning, the Hosts of Heaven rejoiced. For this they were rebuked by God who said that, while Justice was carried out, it was a sad matter, for the Creator did not enjoy the destruction of His creatures. From the Kabbalistic point

Figure 24—PILLARS OF FIRE AND SMOKE
These are the two side columns of the Sefirotic Tree, with Moses holding the central column as leader and direct contact with the Divine. At this point the Israelites were a disoriented, slave-minded rabble. The parallel in an individual is when faced with freedom, without a guide and teaching one can become very confused and lost. The two pillars of theory and practice are there to reveal the straight and narrow path by day and night. (Rev.T. Bankes's Bible, 19th century).

of view we are shown how far into the psyche the body can penetrate and, if we look at the overlapping Trees of the body and psyche, this is borne out by theory and experience. The moment of detaching the body's dominating influence comes when the focus of consciousness shifts Worlds to become principally psychological. This is symbolised by the arrival on the far side of the Red Sea. When the Israelites looked back, not only did they see that their path was now closed by the waters but that dead Egyptians lay on the sea-shore. For a moment the Israelites were stunned by the mortality of these powerful symbols of the flesh. Then they realised that they were free by God's Grace. Through no effort of their own, they had been brought out of the shadow of physical death and into the possibility of immortal life. This occurs when the miraculous opens the eye of the soul in the midst of perhaps great suffering or joy, deep stillness or immense activity to glimpse a view of Paradise and even Heaven beyond the domain of Nature. Thus it was in this moment that Moses and the Children of Israel burst into praises of God singing, 'Who is like unto thee O LORD ... Thou in Thy Mercy hast led forth the people which Thou hast redeemed ... unto Thy Holy Habitation'.

Rebellion and Rules

15. Regrets
Exodus 15-16

Alas, such a moment of triumph and ecstasy has to pass as ordinary conditions begin to assert themselves again. This is shown in the events immediately after the crossing of the Red Sea when Moses led the Israelites into the Wilderness of Shur which means 'to go round about', 'the enemy' and 'lying in wait'. It was here that the full implication of leaving Egypt began to dawn.

Exodus 15:22 says: 'and they went three days in the Wilderness, and found no water. And when they came to Marah, they could not drink of the waters of Marah, for they were bitter'. (Marah means bitter.) 'And the people murmured against Moses'. The reason for this was not just the taste of the waters, the oral tradition tells us, but that when the Israelites saw the destruction of the Egyptians many of them, believing it now safe to return, wished to resume their old life. This condition occurs because it is believed by the uneducated psyche that it is possible to return to old habits with complete impunity now that the body's will has been broken. Moreover, Biblical legend tells us that the sea had cast up much treasure of the drowned Egyptians and because of this many Israelites could not bring themselves to leave the seashore. They were still held by the baubles of the lower World. It was only by Moses's reminding them that it was by God's Grace they were free and safe that he succeeded in persuading them away from the sea and into the desert.

Kabbalistically, Marah and the Wilderness of Shur represent the realisation that on the spiritual journey one can no longer depend upon the support of the physical World. Gone are the myriad props and entertainments that keep the body lulled and the psyche ensnared. The desert is bleak, the prospect awful. There is nothing to look forward to in an already fading afterglow but a great deal of effort and suffering with no guarantee of success. If this be freedom then maybe one should think again. Such a reaction occurs because the ego, perceiving only in terms of its mundane experience, begins to reduce everything into an immediate situation. Thus the waters, in the midst of what appears to be desolation, are indeed bitter when compared with the sweetness of the Nile and its fertile banks.

And Moses 'cried unto the Lord; and the Lord showed him a Tree, which when he cast into the waters made the waters sweet'. The implication of this symbolism is significant to the Kabbalist who sees the Tree as the analogue of Existence whose root is in the World of Emanation, whose trunk is in Creation, whose branches are in Formation and whose fruit is in Action. Thus Grace extends downward to sustain and sweeten the lower levels of the Universe. Such use of analogy illustrates very precisely that the scribes who wove the esoteric teaching into the tribal saga knew exactly what they were about. This is further indicated by the following verses (in the New English Bible translation). 'It was there that the Lord laid down a precept and rule of life; there he put them to the test. He said, "If only you obey the Lord your God, if you do what is right in His eyes, if you will listen to His commands and keep all His statutes, then I will never bring upon you any of the sufferings which I brought on the Egyptians; for I the Lord am your Healer." '

The above (from Exodus 15:25-26) clearly reveals the rules of spiritual discipline. Obey the Teaching and many things that befall the uninitiated through innocence or ignorance will not occur. The sufferings that plague the animal soul will not afflict the seekers after truth because the Lord will be their Healer. This offer is extraordinary in the light of everyday experience but it is borne out by many who have walked the spiritual path. By their centre of attention being in the upper Worlds the saint and the sage are exempted from mundane stress and boredom. Even the beginner finds that Providence watches over him.

The presence of an esoteric teaching is further indicated again in the next verse. When the Israelites came to a place called Elim, which means 'the place of trees', they found twelve springs and seventy palm trees and encamped by them. According to tradition, each of the springs refreshed one of the twelve tribes or spiritual types of human being. The seventy trees refer to the original seventy souls that descended into Egypt. These became, later, the seventy Elders of Israel who guided the people under the direction of Moses and formed the inner council of wise ones within the people. Perceived in personal terms, the seventy are those parts of one's psyche that are sufficiently developed to have some concerted effect on the rest of the organism. Seen on the largest scale, they represent the inner, spiritual level of humanity or, as the Jewish tradition calls them, the House of Israel. In other traditions they are known as the Company of the Blessed, the Communion of Saints and the Great Brotherhood.

From the place of instruction and refreshment at Elim the Israelites moved on deeper into the desert until they came to the Wilderness of Sin which means the 'place of muddiness', of 'hateful passion', 'rage' and 'combat'. Here came the moment when all the regrets and fears that had been held back burst out against Moses as the Israelites murmured, 'Would to God we had died by the hand of the Lord in Egypt when we sat by the fleshpots and when we did eat bread to the full'. The suppressed anger of the lower psyche vents itself on the impulse which seems to have brought it out of an uncomfortable but secure life only to die an even more miserable death.

Fortunately God understood the fears of the Israelites and, while Moses dealt with the panic, Heaven prepared to alleviate the Israelites' hunger and teach them how to follow a simple instruction. The training for the time in the Wilderness was about to begin.

16. Beginning of Discipline
Exodus 16

On the level of individual development, the position of the Israelites so far reflects the following situation. The person has awakened to a way out of the bondage that confines the soul and spirit to the body. These early stages have been made with help from above in the form of a guide who may be seen as an inner or outer teacher. This instructor, aided by Divine Providence, has taken the individual to a crucial point of no return where conscious work has to begin or progress will stop, leaving the disciple stranded in the Wilderness between the bondage of Earth and the freedom of Heaven. The Wilderness is the lower face of the psychological Tree or World of Formation. The psyche, like the Israelites, is composed of a confederation of individual units, families of complexes and tribes of unconscious levels held together by a bond of loose affinities. In the undisciplined there is no developed psychological organisation, only an amorphous mass of elements which, like the Israelites, can be easily swayed and thrown into fear and confusion by strong internal or external factors. To begin bringing about some order within the immature psyche, all esoteric teachings give out apparently petty but strict instructions designed to start the process of real discipline. Naturally these injunctions must be put to the test (remember the forbidden apple); otherwise the lessons inherent in them will not be learnt and greater privileges and duties cannot be given. The function of discipline is to train the will, not only to control the various factions in the psyche but also to contain the concerted power and direct it, under obedience to spiritual law, so that it may be of use to the Creator. Thus the Divine has an interest in the process and will intervene if the teacher's experience is inadequate.

Now the Israelites complained that they would starve in the Wilderness and so the Lord said to Moses that manna would rain down from Heaven; that is, that food would fall from the creative World of the Spirit. Such sustenance is vital to the flagging soul at this stage. However, with this act of Grace came the instruction that the people

Figure 25 — MANNA FROM HEAVEN
Most take for granted what the Universe gives to us. However, at the start of the inner journey it is very clear that we lack psychological and spiritual substance and energy. The Sinai Desert represents this barren part of the process. The Israelites indeed soon complained of being underfed until food came from heaven in the form of Manna. This is a symbol of inner nourishment vital for the soul. (Rev.T. Bankes's Bible, 19th century).

were only to gather a day's supply; and two days' measure on the sixth day.

This was the test to see whether the people could follow instruction—while they were slave-minded from habit, they did possess a free will that must be exercised in this totally new situation.

Moses, as the intermediary between God and the Israelites, told the people that Divine Grace would provide their sustenance, for they had already forgotten that it was the Lord they were dealing with and not Moses. This is a mistake often made by students who see their spiritual teacher as an all-providing parental figure or Divine projection.

According to tradition, manna is created in the third Heaven. This is the place to which a man, during ritual, prayer or contemplation, can rise and receive instruction into the mysteries of Creation. From this spiritual level, called the Heaven of Sincerity, Kabbalah tells us that a pure Light descends to illuminate the twelve tribes. Legend states that the promised manna descended at night, that is into the unconscious state, so that when the people awoke in the morning they perceived its presence in the conscious mind. We are told that the manna took on whatever form of food was most pleasing to the individual. To the child it became milk; to the youth, bread; to the old, honey; and to the sick, like barley soaked in oil and honey.

With the manna came the flocks of quails. If manna represented the right-hand pillar of Mercy, the quails were the left pillar of Severity, as was later to be found when the people gathered them to excess and many died of a plague as a result of their greed (Numbers 11:32-34). However, this degree of severity was not applied at this early stage of discipline when some Israelites gathered too much manna or kept it overnight which they had been forbidden to do. This manna became full of maggots and stank, a warning against taking spiritual things for oneself and the dangers of excess, even in holy matters. It is not unknown for the over-zealous to develop a psychological imbalance when they take too much spirit. Enough for one day is sufficient.

The instruction regarding the manna of the sabbath day is interesting. It tells the student that while he must work at gathering manna to earn merit during the week, the day of rest reminds him to trust the Divine; to realise that he is provided for primarily by Grace. Thus the Israelites were told to devote their time on the Sabbath to study and prayer. Some people, of course, disobeyed and they found nothing, in every sense, on that day.

Moses, himself under instruction, then told the Israelites to keep a measure of manna for future generations, to show how the Lord fed them in the Wilderness after they had been brought out of Egypt. This was done and the manna stored in a container *Lifnay YAHVEH*, 'before the LORD'. This testimony we taste today as we look into the Bible which is a receptacle of the Teaching before the Face of God.

The daily ration of manna was to be supplied to the people all the days they were in the Wilderness, until they came to the borders of the Land flowing with milk and honey. Here it ceased because the fully trained and matured Israelites would then be able to partake directly of the food of Heaven. However, such a state of being was forty years of experience away.

17. Refreshment
EXODUS 17

When the Israelites came out from the Wilderness of Sin, or 'muddy passion' and 'rage', and encamped at Rephidim which means 'support', 'rest' and 'refreshment', there was again no water. This brought out once more the cry of protest. Moses replied, 'Why do you quarrel with me?' '*Ma tenasoon et YAHVEH;*' 'Why do you try to test or challenge YAHVEH?' This is a phenomenon that recurs on the spiritual path when the student is not so much protesting as testing his guide and, indeed, God.

According to rabbinical commentary, when the Israelites failed to keep up their study and practice of the Torah or spiritual teaching, there appeared to be a lack of water. The people, not being able to discern that there was a connection between performance and result, immediately projected their inadequacy on to their leader, saying in their ignorance that it was Moses who brought them out of Egypt and put them in this impossible position. Now the word ignorance can be seen to mean 'to ignore', that is to turn away from what is known, a condition quite different from innocence which is not to know. Innocence is the state of most of mankind. However, those who are spiritually awakened or have experienced the miraculous, as the Israelites did, can distrust, doubt or become ignorant.

Moses, who had learned to curb his anger, prayed for help before the disordered rabble began to stone him. In the individual this would correspond to centring at the Tiferet position of the self and petitioning for help from above to calm the lower unruly elements of the ego. The answer came in the direction to take some of the Elders of Israel, that is, the more mature and stable elements of the psyche, and finding a Rock which hid the living waters. There, the scripture says, they found God waiting. The place was called Horeb which is the same mountain of God where Moses had seen the Burning Bush. Here Moses was instructed to strike the Rock with the Staff of God so that the Elders might perceive that this Rod of Severity which had destroyed the

Egyptians was also the Staff of Mercy by which the people would be nourished. Indeed, folklore says that the Elders were allowed to choose the rock as proof against trickery, because some Israelites, doubting everything irrational or supernatural, suspected that Moses's skill, learnt as a shepherd with Jethro, might locate the water. Rational cynicism is always ready to oppose and test spiritual issues. Moses named the place *Massah* or 'challenge' and *Meribah* or 'dispute' because of this confrontation with God. As the text says, 'Because they tempted the Lord saying, Is the Lord among us, or not?' (Exodus 17:7).

Jewish legend tells us that from this time on the Israelites had an ever-flowing well. This remarkable asset came because of Miriam, Moses's sister, who stands at the Yesodic or ego position of the Children of Israel. She had an intuitive psychic capacity which is common in a highly sensitive ego. The well functioned as long as she lived and symbolises the flow of largely unconscious nourishment such as one might expect to hear from a sensitive but not necessarily wise person or ego. The well, consisting of a rock with holes in it out of which came clear spring water, followed the Israelites through the wilderness, stopping and moving as they stopped and moved. Later, when the Tabernacle was built, it always placed itself opposite the structure and the chiefs of the twelve tribes would petition it to gush forth which it did with such abundance that it brought forth the vegetation that lay hidden in the desert sand to a state of fruition that could feed the tribes.

The Kabbalistic content of this fable is that it describes how the psychic capacity has its limitations because it does not comprehend fully what is flowing through the ego. Sometimes, for example, the mind sees fantasy rather than vision. Nevertheless, although the ego's penetration is not great, it is the spring out through which flow the clear waters of the depths of the soul and spirit. Under discipline the well of the ego refreshes and feeds the person and makes flourish talents that have been hidden in the unfructified terrain of an unwatered psyche. Some legends say that the well only dried up when the Israelites reached Canaan.

Figure 26—BATTLE
Here the Israelites fight with their distant cousins the Amalekites who symbolise the inferior aspects of human nature. When Moses's arms are raised the Israelites prevail and when he lowers them the Amalekites begin to win. He is aided by Aaron and one of the Israelites' chiefs. These represent the secular and spiritual sides of our being that support the Self in this endless struggle. (Rev.T. Bankes's Bible, 19th century).

18. First Battle
EXODUS 17

Because the Israelites had tested God, the Divine sent the Amalekites to attack them at *Rephidim*, the place of Rest. The father of these rapacious tribesmen was Amalek whose name means 'war-like', 'people of prey', 'dwellers in the valley' and 'men of the caves'. These meanings indicate the quality of the tribe and their correspondence to the baser parts of the psyche. The antecedence of Amalek tells us even more. Son of Eliphaz, which means 'gold of God', by a concubine, that is, an inferior liaison, he was the grandson of Esau and therefore the natural rival of the descendants of Jacob. As such the Amalekites were hostile to the Israelites and legend has it that they had waited several generations to take their revenge for Jacob-Israel's assumption of the family birthright. The psycho-spiritual implications are clearly set out here for the first of many battles between the inferior and superior elements in an individual.

Initially, Biblical legend tells us, Amalek could do nothing against the Israelites because of the pillars of cloud and fire. Further, when Moses had uttered the Divine Name in the Amalekites' face, they retreated in disarray. Later, no direct assaults were attempted for the Israelites built an encampment and the Amalekites had to adopt a lying-in-wait strategy, seeking to take the Israelites by ambush and stealth; thus the first stage of psychological order creates the beginning of protection. The other tribes of Sinai and Canaan were naturally interested in the Amalekites' campaign against Israel but did not join in the hostilities as yet. Here we have a perfect description of the interior situation of a person in the early days of spiritual discipline. The Amalekites, or the undisciplined elements closest to the Israelites, seek to disrupt the new order while the deeper old habits, complexes and concepts represented by the Hittites, Hivites, Jebusites, Amorites and Canaanites wait to see if the threat to their territory can be dealt with at the liminal frontier that divides conscious from unconscious. On the psychological Tree this is the line between Hod and Nezah. The vertical

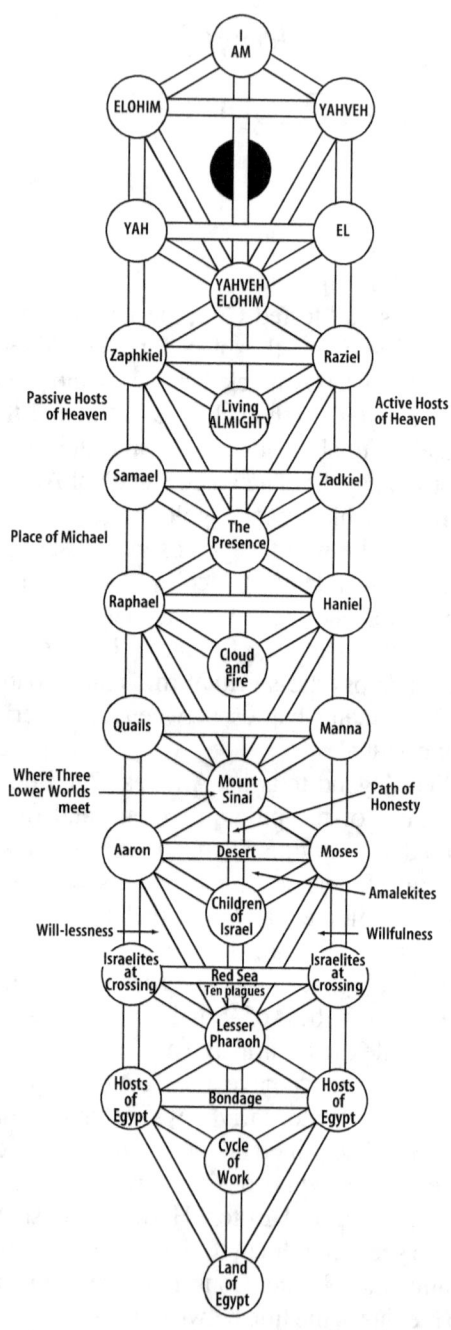

path between the Yesod of the ego and the Tiferet of the self is called—not without reason—'honesty' and 'to lie in wait'.

In the rabbinical story the Amalekites made use of their kinship to the Israelites to draw them out from the protection of the camp, the Amalekites offering to trade favourably with their distant relatives. Thus the inferior elements of the psyche tempt some of the superior but undeveloped parts which are led to believe that business can be transacted harmlessly. The result was not only the death of these Israelites but the mutilation of their genitals by the Amalekites who mocked Heaven by dismembering the covenant of circumcision. The significance of this act is the reduction of psychological will and physical power when the individual's integrity is dishonoured by his own misdemeanours despite the hope that they will not affect his general progress.

At Rephidim, after the testing of God, the Amalekites were allowed to attack openly because the protection of the Divine Cloud had been removed. This Gevuric punishment of the Israelites, however, was not the malice of a revengeful God but the strict chastisement from the far-sighted Divine Teacher. Thus when the Amalekites attacked with swift-moving ferocity, the Israelites were placed in the position of learning how to defend themselves while being taken to task.

So it was that Moses told his servant Joshua, whose name means 'deliverer', to select some strong and disciplined men and go out and fight the Amalekites. This act, for a nation which had lived as a subject people for several centuries, was a crucial turning point in its attitudes as it would be in a person who allowed himself to be dominated by others or by patterns within himself. Legend tells us that Joshua had descended from Joseph, the only one of the twelve sons of Israel who had not sinned. This gave Joshua a distinct advantage but he still needed help because, the legend goes on, the Amalekites possessing magical knowledge knew the most propitious hours to attack. This was because each tribe was under a sign of the Zodiac and therefore vulnerable at certain times. They were not, as yet, united into the House of Israel which, as the spirit, is above the planetary world of Yezirah.

Figure 27—EXODUS
The scale of the operation is shown in this Jacob's Ladder, as it is not only physical but psychological and spiritual. At Mount Sinai the journey begins to take on a new dimension in the purification phase of the Desert. During this period most of the Israelites who had been conditioned by Egypt died off while a new generation, under discipline, were born. In personal development, old habits give way to new and positive attitudes. (Halevi, 20th century).

Thus the Children of Israel could be assaulted at their point of greatest weakness, as often happens in moments of crisis when the psyche is divided.

The aid from above came through the agency of Moses and two other Israelites as he stood on the hill-top overlooking the battle, holding the Staff of God above his head (Exodus 17:9). Seen Kabbalistically, the hill represents a higher level than the field of battle but not too high above the action. The two helpers were Aaron of the tribe of Levi and Hur of the tribe of Judah. Hur means 'noble' (he is also said to be the husband of Miriam, Moses's sister). Thus the two aristocratic families of Israel, representing the lords spiritual and temporal, stood on each side of Moses to support him while he sat upon a stone. This was necessary for, while Israel prevailed when Moses's arms were raised, the warriors fell back when he lowered them in fatigue. Here we have a graphic image of the three pillars of the Tree consciously set up by human will in order to draw down Grace so that Unity might prevail against disunity. This corresponds to a ritual form of Kabbalah in which the individual reaches into the upper Worlds and calls down the Holy Spirit to aid those parts of the psyche that seek unity and cast out the wilful aspects that oppose inner growth.

Moses and his helpers held this ritual form until sunset when Joshua's forces defeated Amalek, 'and put his people to the sword'. In the legends this is done in a clean and honourable manner with no mutilation or humiliation of the enemy. Bad traits, if they must be cut out, should be dealt with like surgery, not butchery, so that there is nothing left to fester.

At the end of this first united action against the forces of evil, Moses records that it is intended to blot out the remembrance of Amalek from under Heaven. That is, the disruptive elements are to be continually removed from the psyche. This intention is made into a memorial after the battle. 'And Moses built an altar and called the name of it YAHVEH-NISSI: for he said, "My oath upon it: the LORD is at war with Amalek generation after generation."'

19. *Teacher Taught*
EXODUS 18

When Jethro heard of all that God had done for Moses and how the Children of Israel had been brought up out of Egypt, he went out to meet his son-in-law encamped at the mountain of ELOHIM. Jethro also wished to see his ex-student because it was clear that he had excelled his teacher. However, such was the love and respect Moses had for his teacher that, accompanied by Aaron and the seventy Elders, he came out of the camp to meet and bow low before Jethro and kiss him in greeting. This tells us much about the relationship between master and ex-pupil. No matter what superior level the younger man might have obtained, he honoured his teacher and the Teaching behind the man that made his spiritual development possible.

When they retired into the privacy of Moses's tent Jethro was told in great detail of all that had befallen Moses since he had left Midian for Egypt. This is common practice; the student relates, in an objective manner, the events of both his interior and exterior life to the Elder, so that the instructor may both learn and teach from the lessons experienced. Jethro was amazed by Moses's report. He exclaimed, 'Blessed be YAHVEH who has saved you from the power of Egypt and of Pharaoh. Now I know that YAHVEH is greater than all the gods'. This last remark reveals the level of Jethro. While according to rabbinical tradition he is not an idolator, he does believe in the pantheistic hierarchy and sees YAHVEH as the greatest of the gods. This is quite different from the monotheistic view and is the dividing point between Jethro and Moses.

After Moses, Aaron and the Elders had shared a meal with him, Jethro offered the sacrifice he had brought to celebrate God's blessing upon their meeting. Then Moses showed Jethro how he operated a court to settle disputes between the tribes and individuals. This took all day, as Moses was teaching as well as assessing cases. Jethro, who was his senior in this experience, observed that Moses was not using his energy economically and advised him to change his working method by delegating work to God-fearing and honest men who could decide the simpler cases. This would leave Moses time to teach and judge the more complex issues.

The significant lesson in the above is that truth comes before everything. While Moses was now more developed than Jethro, he still took advice from his teacher and in a modest way. This must have amazed the Israelites who regarded the aristocratic prophet Moses with some awe. The inner meaning of this passage is that the awakened focus of the psyche, represented by Moses, is inclined to take responsibility for everything; this it cannot do without imposing great strain and loss of time to perform its own special task. One sees this before any learning process becomes automatic. Here Jethro, representing practical and psychological experience, advises the awakened triad of Hod, Nezah and Tiferet to allow those parts of the lower psyche which are trustworthy to take over all the routine work. An example is when the mind allows calculations to be made by learned procedures that can perform perfectly without the conscious attention of the self which has more important work to attend to.

'Moses listened to his father-in-law and did all he suggested'. Thus there were created a set of courts or new complexes in the psyche that dealt with routine matters, so that Moses was only concerned with major issues. After these adjustments, Moses's ex-teacher departed to his own country or level of evolution in Midian.

INITIATION

Figure 28—THE TEACHING

Moses was given the Torah while on the summit of Mount Sinai. He was, by symbolic implication, in a high mystical state of consciousness. Moreover, he spent forty days and nights there, indicating that a whole new process was occurring within him. By this is meant that he ascended Jacob's Ladder and completed a high degree of Self-realisation in which he beheld the Glory of God and received the Teaching. (Rev.T. Bankes's Bible, 19th century).

20. Preparation
EXODUS 19

'In the third month, when the Children of Israel were gone forth out of the Land of Egypt, the same day they came to the Wilderness of Sinai'. This means that the Israelites had passed through three Lunar cycles and had come to the first quarter of the Hebrew year or mid-summer. If the Moon is the symbol of Yesod and the Sun the symbol of Tiferet, the self, then the timing speaks of a crucial event related to the significance of the summer Solstice. In the ancient world, the Solstice was celebrated by a great festival which marked a cosmic moment as the flow of the Universe changed its state in the turning point between seasons. Such an event was considered a transformation in Creation and therefore in the spirit which corresponds to that cosmic World.

The Israelites proceeded into the Wilderness until they pitched their camp before the Holy Mountain. Now the word Sinai means both a high cliff and a deep ravine. This can be seen symbolically as a steep rising-up into the heavens or a profound going-down into the spirit. Here Moses ascended the mount and conversed with God about the House of Israel and the Children of Israel. This is a clear distinction between two levels of Hebrews. The former represents the inner core of Elders, who are spiritually initiated, and the latter, those immature in such matters. Confirmation of this comes as the Lord speaks of how the Divine has borne the Israelites on eagles' wings into the place of the Holy Presence here on the Holy Mountain. This symbol of the eagle is not just poetic imagery but a precise cypher for the Beriatic or Spiritual World; the eagle is one of the four Holy Animals used later in Ezekiel to represent the Four Worlds. According to tradition the Bull symbolises Asiyyah (the physical or action), the Lion, Yezirah (the formative or psychological), the Eagle, Beriah (the spiritual or cosmic) and the Man, Azilut or the Divine. Out of this raising up from bondage comes the possibility of being of real service to God: 'If ye will obey My voice indeed and keep My covenant, then ye shall be a peculiar treasure unto Me above all people.' (Exodus 19:5).

Seen on the individual scale, this is the kind of conversation that occurs deep within the person during the preparation period before an initiation of Commitment. The still small voice presents the offer to the awakening soul as it looks up from the base of the internal Holy Mountain. 'And ye shall be unto Me a kingdom of priests, and an Holy Nation'. Now while this had historic implications for the Jews, it applies equally to the individual as he or she strives to organise the unruly tribes within the psyche into a united whole or Holy Kingdom. All this was said on the mount to Moses who, as representative of the House of Israel, was to transmit the message to the Children of Israel below.

'And Moses came and called for the Elders of the People, and laid before their faces all these words which the Lord had commanded him.' (Exodus 19:7). The Elders, representing the superior aspects of the psyche, agreed that they would do as the Lord commanded. This answer was conveyed, via the intermediary or conscious level of Moses, to the Divine Who replied, 'Lo I come unto thee in a thick cloud that the people may hear when I speak with thee.' (Exodus 19:9). Kabbalistically, this is to say that the Divine Will descends out of Azilut, the World of Pure Light, into Beriah, the World of Air and into Yezirah, the World of Water (which combine to make mist), so that the levels of the lower psyche may experience the Divine Presence.

There follows a detailed instruction on how the Children of Israel must make themselves fit to perceive the Presence of God. They must wash their clothes, that is cleanse their psyches so that no impurity may prevent them from entering a lucid state, and not sleep with their wives, so that the body is quiescent and does not distract the attention. These are practices common to all traditions in preparation for an initiation. The process is to last three days so as to affect the past, present and future. In this way the being is made wholly receptive.

Moses is further instructed to set bounds upon the people not to ascend the mountain. This is to safeguard anyone who thinks he is ready to go up alone and face God—which people with little knowledge and less experience in spiritual matters often want to do. The barriers are also in order to build up physical and psychological discipline, as the abstinence from sex and psychological containment begin to focus their power into a considerable head of pressure. The severe injunctions of stoning or shooting any who break the barriers are more to deter and save the ignorant and innocent from themselves than to punish them. Thus the Israelites were placed into a state of readiness as they awaited the sound of the trumpet call from the Holy Mountain.

PREPARATION

Seen in terms of an individual, here is a person who is about to be taken through an initiation ceremony. He has agreed to a commitment and awaits the moment when he will formally hear the rules of the spiritual tradition and promise to bear witness to them. Such a covenant is not to be taken lightly by anyone; for while such a declaration grants privileges which make the person 'a peculiar treasure' to God, it also means that special duties are to be performed in this transaction between the Divine and man. Because the contract is freely entered into by the individual he is given plenty of time to ponder it as he prepares to undergo the initiation of Sinai, that is a high and deep place between the lower and upper Worlds. The opening solemnity of the occasion is symbolised in Exodus 19:16 by trumpet, thunder and lightning. These sounds and sights from the Holy Mountain generate awe of the Lord which, tradition states, is the first step towards Wisdom.

21. Revelation
EXODUS 19

'And it came to pass on the third day in the morning, that there were thunder and lightnings, and a thick cloud upon the mount, and the voice of the trumpet exceeding loud; so that all the people that was in the camp trembled'. Here begins the initiation into Revelation. Seen on the personal level, the cloud upon the mountain represents the spiritual veil that hides from the psyche the blinding Presence of God as the Divine descends to approach man.

'And Moses brought forth the people out of the camp to meet with God; and they stood at the nether part of the mount'. That is, Moses, the inner guide, drew the psyche out of the framework that protected it against undisciplined elements into a higher state of awareness. In Kabbalistic terms the centre of consciousness was lifted from the ego to come in touch with the lowest point of the spirit at Tiferet, the place where the three lower Worlds meet in the self (Figure 30, page 128).

'And Mount Sinai was altogether on a smoke, because the Lord descended upon it in fire; and the smoke thereof ascended as the smoke of a furnace and the whole mountain quaked greatly'. Here we are shown an image of the whole of a physical, psycho-spiritual organism being shaken by coming into contact with the fire of Azilut.

'And when the voice of the trumpet sounded long and waxed louder, Moses spake, and God answered him by a voice'. This call of a wind instrument indicates that it is Beriatic or Spiritual by nature. Its sustained and increasing volume directs the attention up into a state where man and God can converse. In individual terms the deep and long sounding of a Name of God can take a person up into a state where the speaker and the word spoken become one with the Name and its owner. In this condition Moses spoke and was answered.

'And the Lord came down upon the mount Sinai', that is, the Shekhinah or Divine presence manifested in the upper part of the lower Worlds. 'And the Lord called Moses to the top of the Mount; and Moses went up'. Which is to say that Moses went up into the awakening triad of Hod-Nezah-Tiferet and centred himself in Tiferet which is simultaneously the base of the Spiritual Tree and the top sefirah of the physical World.

'And the Lord said unto Moses, "Go down, charge the people, lest they break through unto the Lord to gaze, or many will perish." ' Here is an often-repeated warning not to allow the untrained to press forward into the realm of the upper psyche and lower spirit lest they become overwhelmed by the experience, as sometimes happens when people force their way into the deeper parts of their being or into the upper Worlds before they are ready. In Hebrew the word for 'push' also means to 'fall', that is to lose that height gained, as many unprepared people do after being blasted by such experiences.

'And let the priests also, which come near to the Lord, sanctify themselves, lest the Lord break forth upon them'. Here even individuals who are familiar with interior experience are warned to fortify themselves. They have to make their wholeness even purer so that they can contain the Divinity that will fill them. In this way the various levels within a person being initiated are symbolised and set in readiness to receive revelation.

The narrative then records how Moses said that the people could not come up because the barriers had been set about the mountain to sanctify it; to make it separate from the mundane which is what the word 'sacred' means. The Divine reply was that Moses should descend and return with Aaron but not the priests. This is significant because it shows that the existing priesthood was not of a sufficiently high level; that is, while an interest in things spiritual is commendable, without real discipline and knowledge there is not the capacity of being to cope with direct experience. Thus, while a person may be well-read and even practise various spiritual methods, these activities can be no more than ego-depth fantasies that could be shattered by entering into the upper Worlds. This dramatic picture of Mount Sinai is not just the witnessing of the power of Creation but contact with the Cause of Causes who, as the Concealed of Concealed, is normally beyond manifestation.

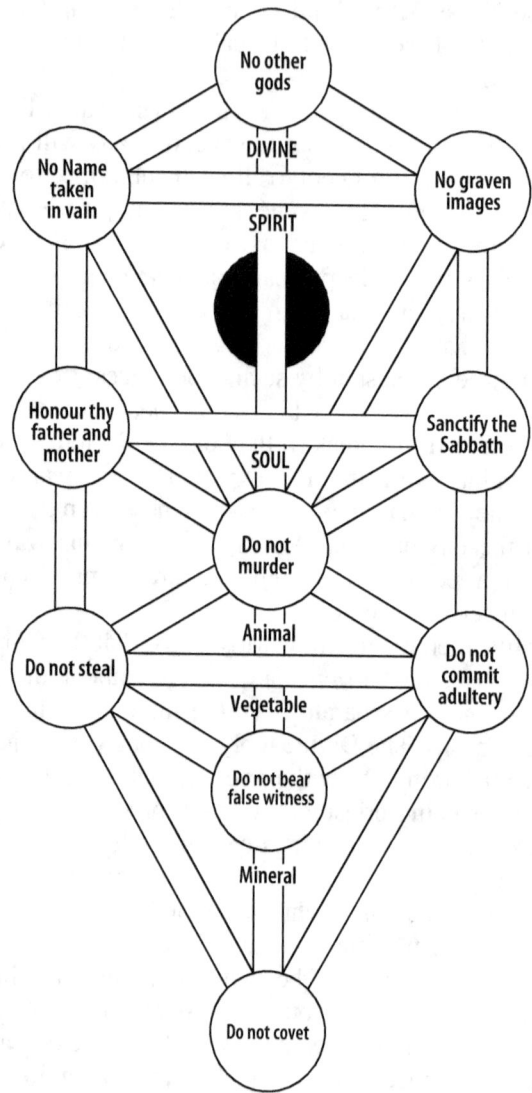

Figure 29 — TEN COMMANDMENTS
As can be seen, the Commandments relate to the sefirot. The topmost triad is concerned with the relationship to the Godhead while the seven lower Commandments are about human conduct. Those of the middle triad speak of honouring one's tradition, setting time aside to consider sacred matters and not to murder one's Self or that of another. The original Hebrew text does not say 'kill' but specifically 'murder'. (Halevi, 20th century).

22. Instruction on Divine
EXODUS 20

'*Vayedabar ELOHIM et Kol hadebareem haaleh laymor*'. 'And ELOHIM spake all these words saying, "I YAHVEH your ELOHIM brought you out of the Land of Egypt, out of the house of bondage."'

Here we see the supernal God Names at the top of the Divine Tree although, in the Hebrew text, the word ANOKI or just 'I' is used instead of the traditional EHYEH to balance the Names of YAHVEH and ELOHIM. Jewish folklore says that Jacob told his children that ANOKI was a familiar term used to Abraham and Isaac and, indeed, it is a more intimate title than is the word EHYEH or I AM. This Name that brought Existence into manifestation was used to Moses at the Burning Bush; but not at Mount Sinai because the Children of Israel could not bear the full majesty of the Divine. The other two major Divine Names traditionally associated with the active, wise and merciful side and with the passive, understanding and just aspect of Divinity are fused into the composite Name YAHVEH-ELOHIM (translated as the Lord thy God) who now proceeds to give forth the Ten Commandments. These follow the sequence of the ten sefirot of the Holy Tree. Beginning with the Crown, the first Commandment states:

'Thou shalt have no other gods before Me'.

This says that only the Absolute must be acknowledged as God. The significance of this utterance, to the ancient world which had innumerable deities, was enormous. It not only gave a base to a nation about to be created for the sole purpose of propagating the idea of a single God but introduced a totally new dimension to the mass of mankind that would affect, in due time, much of the human race. On the individual level this is the realisation that nothing, not even the self, can come before I AM.

'Thou shalt not make unto thee any graven image or any likeness of anything that is in heaven above, or that is in the earth beneath, or that is in the water under the earth. Thou shalt not bow down thyself to them, nor serve them'.

This Commandment is a warning against being caught by the appearance of things. It means that Divinity is not held in an image nor is it to be mistaken for Existence itself because the Absolute is above, below, before and beyond Existence. Even the image of God is only a reflection. God is God and there is no 'thing' like unto God.

'... for I YAHVEH ELOHIM am a jealous God visiting the iniquity of the fathers upon the children unto the third and fourth of them that hate Me. And showing loving kindness to thousands of them that love Me and keep My commandments'.

This passage speaks of the Severity and Mercy extended towards those who ignore or acknowledge Divine sovereignty. The word 'generation' does not actually occur in the Hebrew text but is inserted by translators to make some sense of an apparently incomplete sentence. This suggests that a higher law is being referred to, for the punishment of children would seem unjust and inconsistent. The notion of *Gilgulim* or reincarnation is the most likely explanation. According to this law of transmigration a person takes his rewards and punishments, or Karma, into the next three lives but the mercy of God will extend over thousands. The concept of transmigration is not accepted by all Jews but it has been part of Kabbalistic teaching for many centuries.

'Thou shalt not take the Name of YAHVEH ELOHIM the Lord thy God in vain for the Lord will not hold him guiltless that taketh His Name in vain'.

Here we have the last of the three Commandments concerned with Divinity itself. In this instruction the Names may not be used for any purpose other than addressing oneself to God. To speak of or call upon the Divine without realising whose Name is being used devalues the intimate connection now established between God and man. Such an event is very serious and, therefore, the Lord *in Mercy* gives a warning in Divine Severity to offset taking the Holy Name 'lashav' in falsehood or vanity, the rabbis translate. When placed together these three

INSTRUCTION ON DIVINE

Commandments concerning Divinity constitute man's correct relationship to God.

According to rabbinical tradition, when God spoke of Divinity all the tremblings of the seven Earths below and the seven Heavens above ceased and all the angelic hosts became still, even as all Nature fell silent and did not move. Because of this even the dead and the unborn, we are told, realised that a great event was occurring, as did all the nations of the world who heard the distant resonance of the Divine Decalogue in the language of their own tongues. In this timeless moment the Torah was delivered to the emerging soul and spirit of mankind. Thus it is that all the levels within a human being in this state of revelation become still and listen, each in its own way, to the imparting of instruction concerning first, the relation of man to God and then, that of man to man which now followed.

23. Instruction on Man
Exodus 20

The second phase of the Commandments are concerned with the seven lower sefirot of the Tree. These may be taken to define the external and internal conduct of a community and an individual.

The fourth Commandment, 'Remember the Sabbath, to keep it holy', is placed upon the sefirah of Hesed or the Attribute of Mercy. Thus, after a week of labour the event of the Creator's rest is recognised and set aside as a day to contemplate the purpose of man, the wonders of Creation and to worship God. This act of sanctification allows the expansive aspect of Hesed to fill the Sabbath with loving kindness so that a spirit of openness and ease permeates the day. In this atmosphere both the community and the individual celebrate and imitate the Divine mercy that is said to flow down on the Sabbath through all the Worlds to bring peace even to the inhabitants of Hell on that day.

To 'Honour Thy father and mother' is not only a sign of external respect that creates family stability which is the basis of an ordered social community; it is also an acknowledgement of the sefirot of Hokhmah and Binah, Wisdom and Understanding, known in Kabbalah as the great father and mother. This Commandment, associated with the sefirah Gevurah, states that Judgement should be, with its judicial power, the defender of Tradition and Revelation which are the parents of the Spirit. In the individual this Commandment instructs the sefirah's tendency towards severity to respect the deep inner mother and father of Reason and Inspiration. The correct emotional relationship to Wisdom and Understanding or Intellect holds the psychological balance as this Commandment, based upon Fear of God, is complemented by the Hesedic Commandment, based upon Love of God.

The injunction, 'Thou shalt do no murder', comes from the root word 'ratzach'. This is quite different from 'kill' as it is found in King James's Bible. To kill may be accidental or even necessary, in extreme circumstances, in order to offset a greater evil but to murder is to kill with an evil motive. Besides its obvious social reasons, the esoteric meaning becomes plain when this Commandment is seen to be placed at the Tiferet of the Tree. Here the Teaching shows that one may not destroy one's own or another's self. This is a major crime in that the death of the self affects every other sefirah and breaks the connection between the body, psyche and spirit. Rabbinical tradition states that the first Commandment, at the Crown, corresponds to the sixth of Tiferet. This is borne out in the statement, 'I am the Lord thy God', which is associated with the Crown of every Tree. Thus murder, by bringing about premature physical death, destroys the hope of the psyche and the possibility of growth of the spirit. Such a crime carries great penalties. As one Kabbalist remarked, 'It were better such a person had never been born'.

The two Commandments concerned with adultery and stealing relate to Nezah and Hod respectively. On the Tree of the Commandments they sit upon the two sefirot that act as a bridge between the psyche and the body. Thus the Commandment against adultery is to guard against improper use or mixing of levels as well as sexual irresponsibility. The misuse of acquired powers to bring about a desired effect is a case. Magical charlatanism is a form of esoteric seduction or psychological adultery. The Commandment upon stealing refers to thievery of ideas or emotions as well as physical goods. Spiritual adultery and stealing are to be observed in those who mix and adulterate theory and practice from different disciplines for ego reasons. This not only renders the original teachings impure but also weak and distorted. Many people have destroyed their own and others' possibility of spiritual growth by breaking these two Commandments in the upper Worlds. Such infringements of law are sometimes of greater consequence than their physical counterparts. This leads directly on to the ninth Commandment.

'Do not bear false witness' means to shun lying, not only about one's neighbour but also to oneself. This phenomenon is seen in the ego's relationship at Yesod to the self above at Tiferet. Thus the ego, perhaps inflated by an image of its spirituality, stands before the world and God as a false witness to the Truth. This Commandment is as important as the injunction not to murder and it is set upon the central column which is always related to will. Thus any intention upon this axis of consciousness directly affects the connection with the Divine.

This is why the last Commandment at Malkhut is, in esoteric terms, concerned with the grave sin of denial of the Holy Presence. 'Do not covet' not only applies to another's property but also to coveting that which belongs to God. The bottom-most sefirah is the Kingdom and, as such, contains all the Grace that has come down from above. Thus the Universe and everything in it belongs to the Lord. A human being may borrow, for his time on Earth, those things he is given by Providence but he may not consider them as possessions because they are all gifts. An individual who believes that he is the owner of his property, or even of his body, is deeply mistaken; to covet another's wealth is not only to be deluded but to deny the true source of everything one is or has. This is, in Kabbalistic work, one of the most dangerous misdemeanours because it generates the evil of spiritual pride which caused Lucifer's fall.

The foregoing illustrates the interconnection between all the Commandments as they are set out on the Tree. Rabbinical commentary on the Decalogue draws the commandments together into a Unity so that the breaking of one is seen to affect the others. To Kabbalists this is perceived in both outward social and religious occasions and inward psychological and spiritual manifestation, as events in any World or level must have repercussions in all the others.

The placing of the Decalogue on the Tree not only reveals the principles underlying the commandments but an insight into the sefirot in action. For the Israelites the Ten Commandments were the beginning of real discipline. However, the impact of this discipline was too much for many Israelites who, while wanting divine direction, said to Moses, 'Speak with us, and we will hear, but let not God speak with us lest we die'. Here the untrained tribesmen of the psyche seek to avoid direct contact with reality and seek the shadow of the teacher as they express a fear of death. This, in the individual, is the retreat into the ego which has suddenly become threatened with extinction along with all the old habits and attitudes.

24. Rules
EXODUS 20-23

'And Moses said unto the people, "Fear not, for God is come to prove you, and that His fear may be before your faces, that ye sin not." And the people stood afar off and Moses drew near unto the thick darkness where God was'. According to legend, the experience of being in the Presence of the Divine upon Mount Sinai was so great a strain that the Israelites drew back and down into a distance from the heights. The experience, however, left them with an unforgettable memory, even, we are told, the most ignorant of their number having perceived a vision that many later saints were never to attain during life. Seen at the personal level, here are the lesser parts of the psyche retiring from a deep mystical experience into a lower state of consciousness while Moses remains in touch with the Divine at the place of the self where the lower three Worlds meet.

Folklore says that the Israelites were told they could return to their tents and re-enter into conjugal relations while Moses was told, 'stay thou with Me'. Oral tradition adds that this favour of intimacy granted Moses a clarity that no other prophet was to possess. This was because he was fully awake during his revelations. Here is the difference between unconscious intuition that perceives flashes of insight and full moments of lucid consciousness which relate to a whole spiritual picture. In Kabbalah they are defined as the lesser and the greater states of prophecy. An example of the former is Saul who had ecstatic visions but was unconscious during their manifestation (1 Samuel 10: 10).

While the people retired to resume normal life, Moses held the direct connection between the Divine and human worlds. This began the second phase of the Mount Sinai initiation. It is detailed in the rules that arose out of the ten great Laws of the Decalogue. These regulations came to be called the Book of the Covenant.

The Book of the Covenant is prefaced in Biblical legend by Moses saying that from this time on the Israelites were no longer ignorant. The meaning of this statement is that no action should be performed without its result being considered. The significance of this was to have a profound effect upon the chequered history of Israel in that its periodic acceptance and rejection of Divine law have shown the rest of humanity that while spiritual knowledge means privilege it also means responsibility. It was to demonstrate this principle that Israel was selected to be held in the world's eye.

In order that there should be no misunderstanding of the Ten Commandments when applied to everyday life, the Book of the Covenant sets out a series of examples of correct conduct. To the untrained eye the text from Exodus 21 to Exodus 22:19 seems to be no more than an exercise in legislation. It is not. What is being shown is the application of the Divine principles of Justice and Mercy, based upon a knowledge of the Laws that govern Creation. Thus, for example, 'if a man smite his servant or his maid with a rod and he die under his hand, he shall surely be punished' (or revenged). This is not the harsh law for which the Old Testament is supposed to be famous but a recognition of cause and effect. The crucial word is 'surely'. This does not mean a man ought to be punished but that, by the law of cosmic balance, it is inevitable if the sefirah of Justice is to correct the injustice and bring Existence back into equilibrium.

The rule, 'Not to vex a stranger nor oppress him' but have compassion upon him 'for ye were strangers in the land of Egypt' relates to aiding the seekers after truth, the innocent and those who are confused by the world. One does not take advantage of them. Likewise, the regulation about money lent to the poor is concerned with inner matters. It should not be used to have a hold over them or be lent for gain. This kind of wealth is given to support the weak and not to be corrupted, as often happens when priestcraft enters.

The latter part of the Book of the Covenant is more direct but just as deep. For example: 'Thou shalt not follow the multitude that do evil'. This means do not place oneself under the laws that govern large masses which are for ever subject to the ebb and flow of fashion, mindless entertainment, economic games, politics and war. Evil in this context is Godless activity. A later great teacher in the same tradition said the same thing in the words, 'Be in the world but not of it'. Another verse warns against corrupting justice in favour of a person who is poor but wrong. The truth must come first. This is a warning on the weakness of excessive Hesed or Mercy. In another verse one is advised to rest not only oneself on the Sabbath but one's servants and animals, for all created things must have a period of recreation. This is a profound appreciation of cosmic principles as applied to life.

In the closing verses of the Book, instruction is given upon religious pilgrimages. These are three periods set aside every year for journeys of the spirit. Outwardly these national celebrations are related to the seasons so that a cosmic aspect comes into these periods of spiritual reflection. On the individual level is the daily practice of ritual, prayer and contemplation at dawn, noon and evening. These times of meditation bring the individual and the Universe into relationship and remind one of the Source of Existence.

The Book of the Covenant ends with the statement that the Lord will 'send an angel before thee, to keep thee in the Way and to bring thee into the place which I have prepared'. To the Kabbalist this is the interior connection with the Tradition.

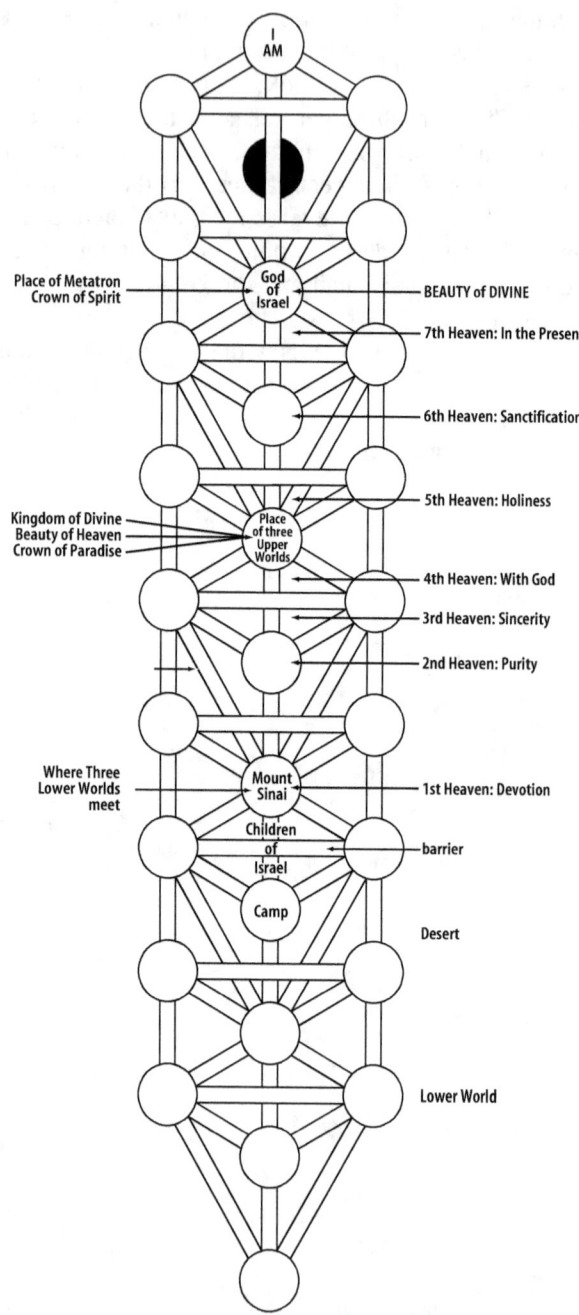

25. Vision
EXODUS 24

According to rabbinic tradition, the angel sent by God to guide the Israelites is none other than the Archangel Metatron who is the transfigured Enoch. The reason for this is the phrase, 'My Name is in him', which is associated with Enoch who, Kabbalistic tradition says, is the esoteric Teacher of Mankind. As such, he has a direct interest in anyone who wishes to rise out of the dominance of the lower Worlds towards the Spirit where Metatron stands at the Crown of the Tree of Creation as the Angel of the Lord. As Enoch or 'the initiated' he knows all the struggles a human being has to pass through and he is, therefore, well qualified to lead the Israelites into the upper and invisible Worlds via the mentor of Moses.

Contact with a spiritual being who gives instruction is accepted in the tradition and many Kabbalists down the ages claim to have been taught by such Maggidim, as they are called. Some are said to have had Elijah as a teacher and this is in order because the prophet, whose name means 'God is YAHVEH', is considered to be a manifestation of Metatron. For one who has reached the level of spirit it is not uncommon to sense the presence of an unseen guide. Many have experienced the intervention of such an intelligence in their lives, although no direct proof of these things can be established except through personal experience. An example in Kabbalah is Rabbi Joseph Karo, a lawyer living in sixteenth-century Palestine, who recorded in his diary what his angelic mentor told him.

The direct contact with the angelic levels reveals a major change of state in which intercourse between Heaven and Earth can now freely

Figure 30—LADDER OF MOUNT SINAI
With their camp at the equivalent of the ego, the Israelites ascend to the foot of the Holy Mountain. Here, where the three lower Worlds meet, they remain while the Elders or higher parts of the psyche and Moses go on. At the level of the fourth Heaven, Elders pause while Moses continues up. From the Crown of Formation the Elders experience the Awesomeness of Creation and the Divine Glory while Moses communes with the Holy One. (Halevi, 20th century).

occur. The significance of this, to Israel and the individual, is enormous. Seen kabbalistically, it means that the celestial regions of existence can manifest below in a consciousness that is capable of receiving power and a vision of what normally cannot come into mundane experience, while it enables those who are below to ascend out of the earth-bound condition and glimpse the wonders of the upper Worlds. It is at this point in Exodus 24 that an invitation is extended, not only to Moses but also to Aaron, his two sons and the seventy Elders, to come up into the higher reaches of the Holy Mountain.

At the altar of twelve pillars, built by Moses below the Mountain, the Book of the Covenant was read out. After the people had consented to do everything asked of them, Moses sprinkled the blood of the sacrifice over them saying, 'Behold the blood of the covenant which the Lord hath made with you in agreement of all these words'. By this physical and symbolic operation the covenant was made and sealed, for rituals are enacted so as to affect the body, psyche and spirit of the covenanter. In this manner all levels and Worlds are involved and the consent is total. Having completed the ceremony, the heightened state of consciousness allowed those invited by the Divine to ascend up through the Worlds. This miraculous journey is described in Exodus 24:9-11 with the greatest brevity. 'Then went up Moses and Aaron, Nadab and Abihu and the seventy Elders of Israel. And they saw the God of Israel and there was under His feet as it were a paved work of sapphire stone and as it were the body of Heaven in clearness. And upon the nobles of the Children of Israel He laid not His hand and they saw the ELOHIM, and they ate, and they drank'.

In Kabbalistic terms, the company of souls reached the Crown of Formation which is simultaneously the Central Tiferet of the World of Creation and the bottom sefirah of Emanation.

From this place where the three upper Worlds meet they saw the Divine Light of Azilut shining through the lucid substance of Heaven above which stood, with His feet touching Creation, the God of Israel. While in this gracious state none came to any harm that might have been incurred in the presence of such spiritual power and Divine radiance. Instead they were fed with the food of the angelic beings that is the Emanation of the ELOHIM.

Seen in personal experience, such a moment of vision during an initiation ceremony is not unknown, although it may be only the briefest of flashes that reveals all the Worlds present within and without a person. This brevity, as in the scripture, is to safeguard against any danger to an unprepared psyche and body. In some cases the person wishes to die because the soul and spirit yearn for nothing else but union with God. While some traditions seek this state as an ideal, Kabbalah does not train its practitioners to leave the Earth before their time. It takes the individual up to this level in order that he might become a channel for the higher Worlds to flow through and down in what is called an act of unification. In this way the lowest levels of Existence may be permeated with a consciousness of soul, spirit and Divinity.

It is interesting to note here that the sons of Aaron are included in this ascension because later they were to die when they used 'strange' or alien fire in a priestly offering (Leviticus 10:2). This warns the spiritually ambitious that even though one may be privileged there is still danger of mistakes. This can cost the greatest price and precipitate a fall from the highest place most mortals can reach.

26. Ascent
EXODUS 24

'*Vaal Mosheh el haHar*'. 'And Moses went up into the mount, and a cloud covered the mount. And the Glory of YAHVEH abode upon Mount Sinai and the cloud covered it six days; and the seventh day He called unto Moses out of the midst of the cloud'. In this series of majestic sentences Moses begins to ascend beyond the level of the Elders and enter the next World. Seen Kabbalistically, he rises out of the Crown of the World of Formation to enter the Place of Beauty which lies at the centre of the World of the Spirit. This Tiferet of Creation is the midstage of the place where the three upper Worlds meet and traditionally where the great archangel Michael, whose name means 'Like unto God', resides as the priest on high in the heavenly Jerusalem. At such a spiritual level one is said 'To be with God' although the translation through to the third or Azilutic stage of this level, into the Malkhut-Kingdom of the Divine World, is yet to come.

In apocryphal literature, the space between Moses leaving the Elders and going up into the higher part of the mountain is filled by an account of this stage of his ascension. It is not unlike his experience at the Burning Bush; but the difference is that it is not an immature Moses although he is by no means absolutely self-confident as he traverses the various thresholds of the Heavens. This tells us that while one may be secure about the levels below, even be master of them, there are always the levels above which test the balance, purity and knowledge of those who penetrate these highest Worlds. That is why certain kabbalistic practices were reserved only for those who had good health, a stable psyche and a well-established connection with the spirit.

In this ascension, we are told, the cloud that lay upon the crest of Mount Sinai opened for Moses to enter. Kabbalistically, this highest cloud represents the watery and airy levels of Formation and Creation containing the Presence of the Holy Spirit. As Moses passed out of sight of the Elders below, that is, the psychological World of Yezirah and into the spiritual realm of Beriah, he was met by the angelic porter

Kemuel who, with twelve thousand angels of destruction, guarded the gates of the firmaments. This formidable being demanded of Moses why he was there where it was not right for a man to be? Moses replied that he had been called by the Holy One to receive the Torah and take it back down to Israel. Kemuel, like all angelic beings, could only carry out one order at a time and still blocked the Way. And so, we are told, Moses was given the power to remove Kemuel completely from that World and so continue his ascent which passed through seven stages. This is hinted at in Exodus 24:16 in the words, 'For six days and the seventh day He called Moses out of the cloud'. During these days Moses goes through a series of similar encounters with other angelic beings, each one fiercely questioning his right to be there and to go higher. Fortunately the All-Knowing One is watching over the ascent and so the Way is cleared for Moses. It is interesting to note here that once the angels have accepted Moses they become his protectors. The angel Hadarniel, for example, runs before Moses to the next stage of Sandalphon who binds the prayers ascending from below into garlands for the Lord's Crown. This angelic occupation is so important that the Heavenly Hosts quake as the braided prayer rises out of the lower realms. To illustrate further the other-Worldliness that Moses traverses in his ascent, at one point he has to cross the fiery river of Rigyon where the angels purify themselves. This fierce-burning stream surrounds the Throne of Heaven as a celestial moat and forms part of a spiritual topography described in early kabbalistic literature.

As Moses approached the Throne he was met by the archangel Raziel, the revealer of God's secrets, who brought Moses safely through the angelic ranks of the Throne and into the Presence of the Divine. The scriptures describe the sight of the Glory of the Lord like devouring fire on the top of the mountain. The oral tradition, in contrast to this severe aspect of the Divine, says that Moses beheld God seated on his Throne ornamenting the Teaching with crown-like decorations, to indicate how elaborate the Torah would become in later times. Here Moses remained for forty days while the Holy One personally instructed him on the nature of Divinity, the composition of the Universe and the purpose of mankind. Moses was also shown what could be set down in writing and what must only be passed on by word of mouth. Out of this came the Written Law, which was to be studied during the day where it could be seen, and the Oral Law which was to be studied at night in discreet seclusion. Moses was also shown all over the seven Heavens and allowed to see the celestial Temple.

Jewish folklore records that Moses kept forgetting his lessons, a common experience for anyone going through a mystical experience. However, he was reassured that the Teaching was deeply embedded within the spiritual levels of his nature. At the completion of his celestial training course he was given two tablets made of a strange sapphire-like stone that could be rolled up like a scroll. On to these had been engraved the Ten Commandments in such a way that they could be perceived from both sides. Moreover, between each line were written all the particulars of the precepts. This instrument, written by the Divine finger, was to form the basis of the Bible as we know it.

Besides the laws to order and govern the as-yet unorganised community of tribes, Moses was given detailed instructions for building a movable Tabernacle. These not only included plans for the structure but the designs for furniture and priestly vestments. These were meticulously worked out before being imparted to Moses because the Divine wished every detail to reflect an aspect of the Torah or Teaching upon Man, the Universe and God.

All the foregoing, when seen on the level of the individual, is the experience of the deepest realisation. In such a moment what was, what is and what shall be for oneself is revealed in a profound illumination in which all the apparently unconnected events of life fuse into the recognition that one has been trained to fulfil a certain destiny. This usually precipitates a total re-orientation deep within as one is shown things about the upper Worlds hitherto only heard about. As with Moses, the result is usually the receiving of a direct instruction on how to bring down what has been shown in vision and thus build a Tabernacle on Earth to act as a living reflection of Creation and Divinity.

Knowledge of Existence

27. Readiness
EXODUS 25

The twenty-fifth chapter of Exodus opens with the words, 'And the Lord spake unto Moses saying, Speak unto the Children of Israel, that they bring Me an offering; of every man that giveth it willingly with his heart ye shall take My offering'. This statement by the Divine before the description of the pattern of the Tabernacle is crucial in that it says that a man must give the Lord something of his heart. In Kabbalah this is the triad of the Soul, composed of the emotional sefirot of Justice and Mercy, or discipline and love, and Tiferet the sefirah of Beauty and Truth.

In rabbinical tradition God says, 'Do not think you are giving these gifts in repayment for the things I did for you in Egypt, when I clothed and shod you by the Egyptian who heaped gifts upon you. No! You shall give your contributions towards the sanctuary because you wish to'. This statement sets up a correct understanding of wealth and its proper use, thereby defining the way in which an individual should apply his physical skills and psychological gifts to aid in the growth and building of an inner spiritual sanctuary.

The text then goes on to make out a list of materials. They are gold, silver and brass; blue, purple and scarlet dyes; fine linen, goats' hair, rams' skins, red dye, badgers' skins and shittim wood, oil, spices, onyx and other stones to be used in the priestly garments. The fact that the Israelites were deep in the desert clearly indicated that they had to draw upon their own resources. The psychological parallel is exact. In work on the Soul a person cannot rely on anyone else, nor can he borrow or even steal anything that will enhance him.

The materials listed have esoteric significance. For example, gold which is to be worked into a fine state represents lower Emanation while ordinary gold symbolises the World of Creation. Silver symbolises the World of Formation and brass the World of Action. The various colours likewise symbolise the three lower levels of Existence. Sky blue is for Heaven; purple, the mixture of blue and red, for the World

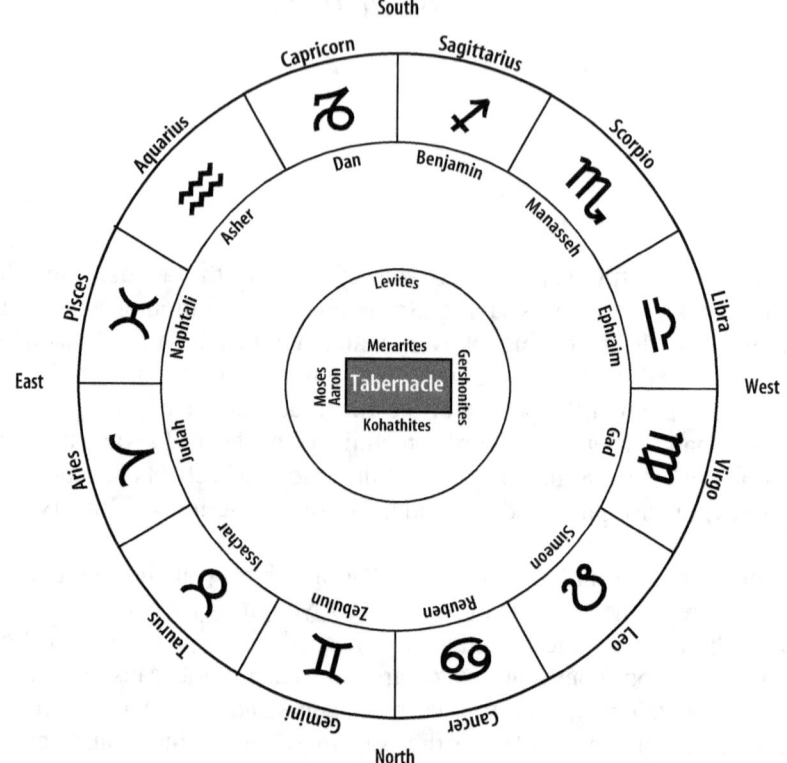

Figure 31 – TRIBES
According to tradition, the twelve tribes were placed in a circle around the Tabernacle, in the order of the Zodiac. This idea dates back to Abraham who came from Ur of the Chaldees, called the city of astrologers. Each tribe is related to a particular Sign according to its nature. For example, Judah the warrior clan was under Aries while Dan, which means Judgement, was seen as Capricornian. The Levites, as the priestly clan, were believed to be above the influence of the stars. (Halevi, 20th century). Publisher's Note: *the drawing is based on the classic astrological chartwheel which reverses the compass points.*

of the Soul and scarlet, the colour of blood and earth, for the World of Action. The white linen is the base material and colour for the Divine Ground of Emanation.

The site of the Tabernacle is to be at the hub of the Israelites' camp which is to be arranged according to the four divisions of the twelve tribes or human types. These subdivisions are expressed by the four elemental temperaments associated with the four Worlds. Here, Action is represented by Earth, Formation by Water, Creation by Air and Emanation by Fire. Thus the surrounding circle to the nucleus of the Tabernacle is to be cosmic in conception. As said, each tribe at this point had a sign of the Zodiac (Figure 31). According to rabbinical tradition the standards of the tribes Juda, Issachar, Zebulon, Reuben, Simeon, Gad, Ephraim, Manasseh, Benjamin, Dan, Asher and Naphtali were arranged in their Zodiacal sequence.

On the inside of the tribes, between them and the Tabernacle itself, were to be the priestly tribe of Levi. These, in turn, were divided into four clans of Merari to the south, Gershom in the west, Kohath to the north and Moses and Aaron and his sons in the east. This honour was because the tribe of Levi had carried out the precepts of the patriarchs throughout the bondage in Egypt, thus keeping alive the memory of higher Worlds while the other Israelites copied the customs of the Egyptians. This loyalty to the God of their forefathers earned them the privilege and duty of guarding and serving the sanctuary. Moses was of this clan and, by becoming its leader, inevitably ruled the other tribes as chief priest and king of Israel in all but name. His early training in the Egyptian court and with Jethro had been carefully fated by providence.

Seen on the individual level, the arrangement of the camp represents the idea of an ordering of the outer psychological elements according to the Zodiacal temperament of each tribe. The more refined and deeper aspects of the psyche formed by long and diligent devotion (the Levites) make up an inner place in relation to work and worship. This interior layer is composed of those parts of us that have combined to give the psyche the beginning of some unity and stability. These interior Levites come easily under spiritual discipline while the outer circle of Israelites are quickly distracted by external matters or inter-tribal conflicts within the psyche. The division of the Levites into four clans reveals the four traditional approaches of ritual, devotion, contemplation and mysticism. Here were the ways of action, emotion and intellect with the clan of Aaron to represent the mystical dimension.

According to the Talmud the space at the centre of the circle of

Israelites is to be the site of the Tabernacle. This is not only to be the focus of the Divine on Earth but the centre of Holiness for all the nations of the world. There now follows the specification for the *Mishkan* or place of the Dwelling where the Holy Shekhinah can reside.

28. Divinity
EXODUS 25

The ninth verse of the twenty-fifth chapter of Exodus records God's words: 'According to all that I shew thee [the Creative World of Ideas] after the pattern of the Tabernacle, and the pattern of all the instruments thereof [the Formative World of Shapes], even so shall ye make it [The World of Action]'. The next six chapters of Exodus are concerned with an exposition of exactly how the operation is to be carried out. The human parallel is the sculptor who wills a creative idea into a design which he can execute as a solid work. Here is Will, Creation, Formation and Action. Thus man, the image of the Creator, imitates God.

In the Divine instructions to Moses, everything had been worked out to the finest detail. Each element related not only to its neighbour but to a larger unit which in turn fitted into an integrated scheme that expressed within its complexity the Unity of Existence. To conceive, design and build such an edifice required very exacting specifications and these were given out according to the processes of manifestation. Thus it is that the creation of the Tabernacle does not begin with the outer overall plan but the innermost and smallest element. The jewel is made before the setting. Following the Laws of Existence, the Ten Commandments are to be placed in an Ark; that is, the Divine representatives of the sefirot are to be contained by a creation symbolising both space and time.

The Ark, which was, after the Tables of the Law, the most sacred of objects, was to be an oblong chest two and a half by one and a half by one and a half cubits. Its base was to be made of unknotted and unfissured shittim wood which, tradition tells us, Jacob had taken down into Egypt to be held in readiness for such use. The casket of wood was to be overlaid with gold. This luminous and unchanging quality was used to express the Eternal Sovereignty of God. Metal of the Sun, gold, was endless light held in material form. Sheathing the wooden Ark inside and out, the interior and exterior caskets spoke of hidden and manifest Emanation. To complete Azilutic symbolism, Moses was instructed to make a crown of gold that was to act as a halo of radiance round the top edge of the Ark.

The lid of the Ark was to be a slab of pure gold, two and a half cubits long by a cubit and a half deep. This was to be the Mercy Seat. Seen kabbalistically, the Seat represented the upper part of Creation which corresponds to the lower part of Emanation. This is where the Divine World interpenetrates the World of Spirit. At either end of the Seat were to be set two Cherubim made out of beaten gold whose wings arched up and over the Seat to form a Throne. These angelic creatures of the upper Worlds, whom God set to guard the Way to the Tree of Life, were to flank the Holy Presence of the Shekhinah that was to hover between them and over the Ark. As such they represented the Hosts of YAHVEH on the right and the Hosts of ELOHIM on the left. This arrangement laid out the scheme of the three pillars, Mercy on the right, Justice on the left with Divine Grace in the middle. Kabbalistically, here are the three supernals of Creation with the CREATOR backed by the great spirits of Raziel and Zaphkiel. It was not without reason that the Ark was called the Throne of Heaven. Later it was to be covered with a drape of sky-blue fabric when it was transported by the Levites. According to folklore the overall spread of the Cherubim was twenty-two spans. This is the number of the letters in the Hebrew alphabet. In Kabbalah the letters define the paths on the Tree that join the sefirot. They also, according to tradition, bring Creation into being by their combinations. Another fragment of folklore says that the Cherubim had their faces turned back as if looking at their Teacher. The Bible is more precise, in that the text declares that their faces shall be set towards the Mercy Seat where the Lord promises to dwell and meet with Moses.

The Ark was to be the place where the Divine reached down through the Worlds to talk with man. In front of this Earthly altar an individual could address his Maker, who was prepared to come out of Absolute Transcendence into the relative Universe so as to speak directly to a human being 'as a man speaks to his friend'. Such an event had the most extraordinary implications for all mankind. Indeed, the Ark would not only be the centre of the Tabernacle, the Israelite camp and the surrounding nations but also the focus of Creation as the Divine communed with man, the Image of God in the midst of Existence.

29. Creation and Spirit
EXODUS 25

After the Ark comes the description of how to make the Table of the Showbread. This is to be constructed of shittim wood which is then encased in pure gold. Like the Ark, it is to have a crowned border. The Table is to be set on the north side of the Tabernacle. Upon it is to be placed twelve cakes or loaves of bread baked of fine flour and these are to be left there for a week in the Presence of God. After that they are to be taken by the priests and eaten in a holy place while twelve more fresh loaves are to be set in their place on the Table. Also to be made with the Table are a set of utensils to be used to prepare the sacred meal. This meal has two levels. It speaks of the sustenance given to all creatures who dine at Creation's royal table and of the Divine Host who provides everything. Thus while the Showbread comes from the earth, the vessels of gold are never to be filled with any Earthly produce as they are regarded as the Heavenly contribution to the repast. The beauteous setting-out of the Table may be seen as man's offering to God Who, we are told, takes pleasure in the service provided by the priestly representatives of mankind.

The next object to be discussed was the Menorah or seven-branched candle-stick. This was to stand opposite the Table of the Showbread in the south. It was to be constructed of pure gold and beaten out of one piece. Its form was to be a central shaft with three arms on either side, thus making seven candle-holders in all. Its decorations were to contain twenty-two elements, so that it became not only a beautiful ritual implement but a metaphysical diagram of the Laws of Existence. This is seen in the following way. The central light is the Crown of Grace with merciful or active lights on the right wing of the lamp standard and the severe or passive lights on the left (Figure 32). The three joining points of the arms on the central shaft of Equilibrium fix the places of Knowledge, Beauty and Foundation with the tripod base as the Kingdom. The twenty-two specified decorations correspond to the twenty-two paths of the Tree that connect the sefirot. The scripture

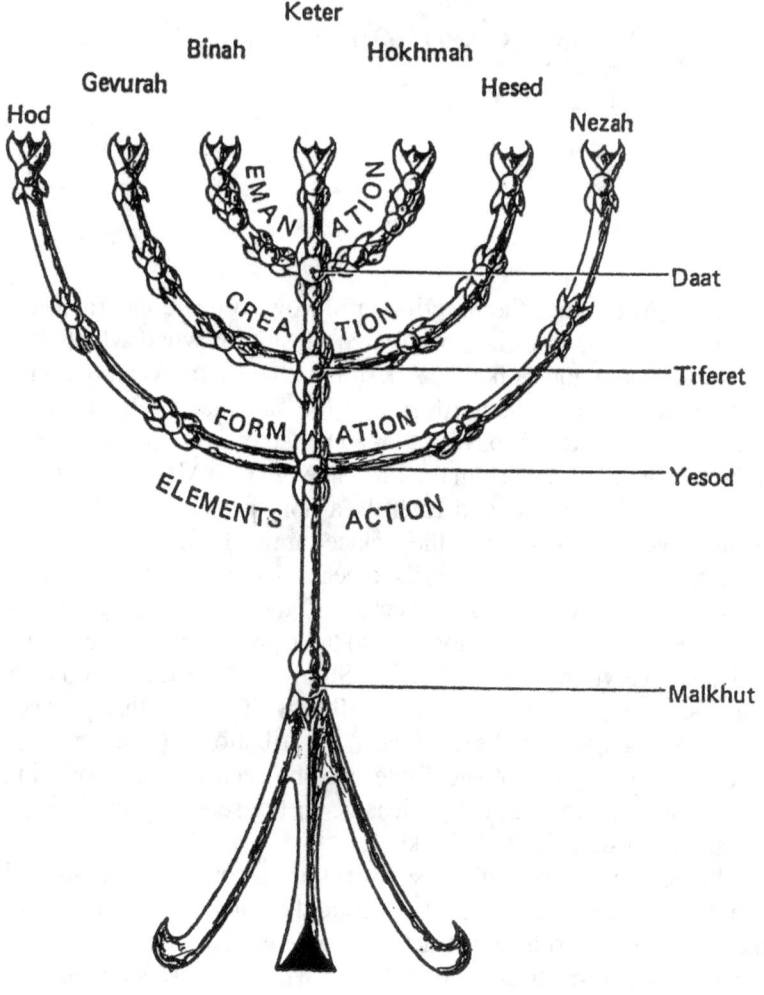

Figure 32—MENORAH
Beaten out of a single piece of untarnished gold, to represent the purity of the highest Realm, this seven-branched candlestick depicts the ten sefirot. The right and left wings symbolise the pillars of Mercy and Justice with the central column being that of Grace. The twenty-two decorations relate to the Paths and Hebrew letters while the base echoes the three basic principles that govern Existence. Also to be seen are the spaces of the four Worlds. (Halevi, 20th century).

(Exodus 26:30) is absolutely insistent that the design revealed upon the mountain shall not be deviated from. There must be no human distortion of this precise model of the Teaching.

When the Table of the Showbread and the Candelabrum are placed together they form a unit, the Lamp throwing light upon the sacred meal that is to be set before the veil of the Ark. Seen kabbalistically these two symbols may be regarded as the two lowest side sefirot of the Beriatic Tree and simultaneously as the two uppermost side sefirot of the Yeziratic World. The Table on the right is the Active giving of sustenance and the Lamp on the left the formulation of the Tradition. These qualities and functions apply to Beriatic Nezah and Hod and the Yeziratic Hokhmah and Binah. Beyond and above the Ark is the Mercy Seat which completes the upper triad that places the Throne of Heaven below the Divine Man of Ezekiel's vision.

The inner meaning for the individual of these sacred objects is that they represent the corresponding levels of a person. The Ark is that part of ourselves in which the Divine dwells unseen and often unknown. It is the place where our spirit comes before the Holy One within while the Table and Lamp symbolise the hidden springs of spiritual sustenance and support. However they, like the Ark at this point in the scriptures, are yet to be realised. This stage has not been reached because as yet there is no firm psychological organism or stable physical discipline to manifest these spiritual principles in form and materiality. The design and construction of the Tabernacle and the surrounding court which represent the lower parts of Creation, all of Formation and the upper parts of the realm of Action symbolise the spiritual, psychological and physical vehicles to be developed within the individual.

The situation being described for the individual is that the higher developed part of him, embodied by Moses, is under the process of deep instruction. However, there is as yet no connection between the upper and lower levels of consciousness. There is theory but no application, revelation but no comprehension. Direct knowledge is present but there is as yet no way of bringing it into ordinary life. The Elders of the upper psyche wait below but out of sight and the Israelites of the lower psyche remain far away at the foot of the Mount. The levels are there but unconnected. The marriage between the Worlds has yet to be accomplished. This is set out symbolically in the next sequence.

30. Worlds within Worlds
Exodus 26

The instructions for the making of the Tabernacle begin not with the wooden framework but with ten curtains which represent the ten sefirot of the World of Formation. These are to be made of the white of the linen woven with blue, purple and scarlet thread which symbolise the four levels of Divinity, Creation, Formation and Action within the Yeziratic World. The coupling of the curtains, the way they are meant to hang down from the top and on either side, speaks of the three pillars, and the joining of them all into a whole signifies the unity of that World. The Cherubim woven into the fabric indicate that this is the realm of the angelics

The second, third and fourth layers of goat, ram and porpoise skins over the linen curtains may be seen not only as a protection against the elements but also as the three outer or lower parts of Formation as it comes into direct contact with the physical World of Action. Made of the skins of a high mountain animal, a beast of the pastures, a creature of the sea, they describe the hierarchy of levels that shield the inner curtains. The eleventh panel of seals' skin which forms the fold over the front of the tent could be regarded as the place where the lower three Worlds meet beyond the screen that will stand before the entrance to the Tabernacle.

The wooden construction of the Tabernacle is overlaid with gold inside and out, indicating the connection between the World of Formation and the Divine World of Emanation; the Keter (Crown) of Formation comes into contact with the Malkhut (Kingdom) of Emanation at the Tiferet of Creation. In human terms this is where the psyche touches the Divine at the centre sefirah of the spirit. The design of the Tabernacle allows it to be erected and dismantled at will. This has an esoteric significance for it describes how an individual in the midst of physical labour, psychological activity and spiritual work can set up a sacred place in which to perform his acts of worship, meditations or contemplations. The setting-up and striking of the interior Tent of the Tabernacle occurs every day in the life of a person on the inner journey to the Holy Land.

The precise proportions of the Tabernacle are clearly not without reason. According to the specification, the Holy of Holies is a perfect cube which describes the six directions of Existence. This tells us that the Holy of Holies containing the Ark represents lower Emanation as manifest in the upper half of the Creative World. The upper part of Divinity is represented by the presence of the Shekhinah hovering between the wings of the Cherubim. The double length of the Sanctuary indicates that the lower part of Creation and the upper part of Formation are contained by the double cube.

The Tabernacle's symbolism is completed by the Veil that divides the Sanctuary from the Holy of Holies and the Screen at the Tent's entrance which separates the Tabernacle from the court and beyond.

The Veil before the Holy of Holies is again made of white, blue, purple and scarlet linen and yarn with Cherubim woven into it. This rich hanging is draped from four shittim-wood posts covered with gold. Here again we get the repetition of the four levels of Divine Will, Divine Mind, Divine Heart and Divine Action that hold Existence in being. The Veil itself, besides repeating this motif, seals the Holy of Holies into a complete darkness and so the Shekhinah dwells out of the sight of man, except when the High Priest enters the Holy of Holies on special holy days. The significance of this to the individual is that the Holy of Holies represents the innermost place of his unconscious where the interior Ark of God resides. When on some special occasion the high priest or Divine contact within a person is aroused, his consciousness may enter into that space at the deepest level of his being and come into his own Holy of Holies. Here he may commune in the still silence of complete darkness with God Who has no image.

The five posts at the entrance of the Tabernacle may be seen as symbols of what are known in Kabbalah as the five gardens (Figure 34). These are formed on the extended Tree of Jacob's Ladder by the five kite-like configurations of sefirot known as faces. These five gardens beginning at the bottom represent: 1. the lower Earth; 2. upper Earth and lower Eden; 3. upper Eden and lower Heaven; 4. upper Heaven and lower Emanation; and 5. upper Emanation. They may also be seen as representing the five lowest sefirot of the Tree of Creation with the four posts before and beyond the Ark representing the upper sefirot; the Crown of that World is seen as hidden in the Holy of Holies itself.

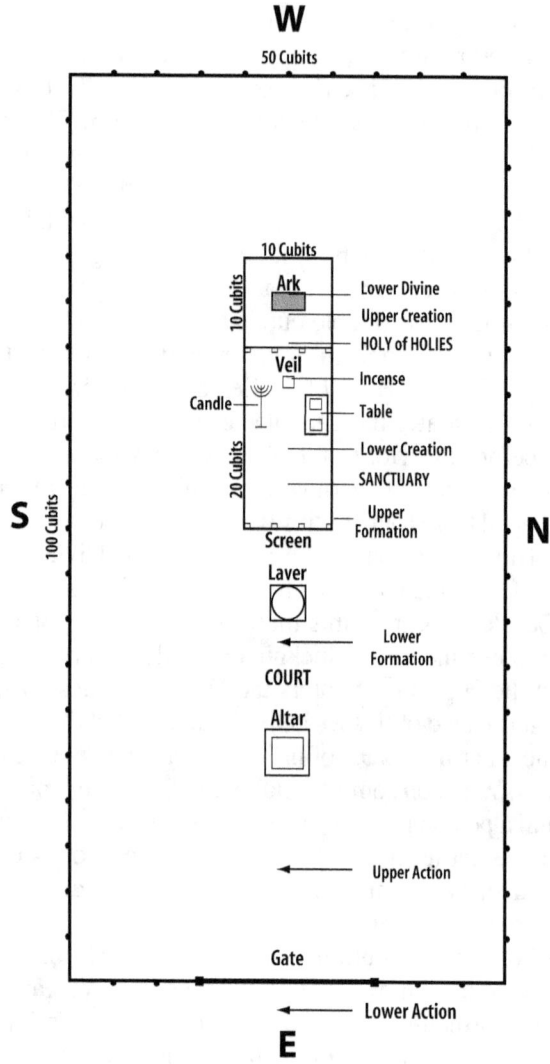

Figure 33 – TABERNACLE LAYOUT
The plan of the Tabernacle sets out the scheme of the four Worlds. The Ark is the lower level of the Divine represented by the Holy of Holies which is also related to the upper part of Creation. The Sanctuary symbolises the lower portion of Creation which corresponds to the upper section of Formation. The Court, above the Altar, is the lower level of Formation which matches the upper section of Action. Outside the precinct is the lower portion of Action where the Israelites are encamped. (Halevi, 20th century).

The whole of the Tabernacle may be perceived as a beautifully designed set of interwoven symbols of both the upper Worlds of the Universe and the inner levels of man. Its order and composition are so carefully set out in the scriptures that we must conclude that nothing is without reason; even planks, bars, sockets and rings having an inner significance. While we may never know the full picture, for scholars say that details have been lost or added later to the text, we can still recognise the esoteric basis of this building upon which Solomon based his Temple.

For the individual the meaning of the foregoing is that one has to construct a Tabernacle within one's being; bring forward the offerings of the body and psyche and form, according to a spiritual design, an inner place wherein the Soul and Spirit can come into correct relation to the Highest in the Holy of Holies. However, while this inner part is being constructed, the outer court surrounding the Tabernacle has to be built so that there is a flow between the upper and inner and the lower and outer Worlds.

31. From Heaven to Earth
Exodus 27

Before the court of the Tabernacle is specified in Exodus the design of the Altar is set out. This is to be made of shittim wood but covered with bronze. The use of this less precious alloy of tin and copper not only denotes the lower Worlds but also the inter-penetration of the upper physical World and the lower World of Formation. Bronze is used throughout the court, even down to the pegs that hold up the outer posts.

The Altar itself also contains the principle of the four Worlds in its four corner horns. Below, inside and midway from the base, the Altar has a grating. This position is not just a practical level for the burning process but a very precise statement about the junction between Worlds, for it is here that the fire trans-substantiates the offerings from a physical solid into liquid fat, then a vaporous smoke that ascends up to the Divine. The method of sacrifice may seem primitive to modern man but we must accept it as the outer custom of that time and perceive the inner meaning. The giving of the best produce for sacrifice was to transform it from the profane into the sacred so that whatever was sacrificed was as much to its own benefit as well as the sacrificer's. The alternative was for the animal to be killed for the dinner table.

In the initial instructions to Moses on the Mountain there is no mention of the Great Water Laver, nor is there any mention of the altar of incense before the curtain of the Ark in the sanctuary of the Tabernacle. These verses are considered by some scholars to have been added after the Babylonian Exile. Their purpose is the purification of the priests and the raising of the level of the celebrants' conscious state by the use of incense. Tradition has it that the Laver for ablution was made out of the metal mirrors of the women who ministered at the door of the Tent of Meeting. Symbolically this idea clearly represents the dissolving of the ego's vanity and its transformation into an instrument for obtaining purity; and this is the exact role of the sefirah Yesod in the psychological World of Formation.

The outer walls of the Court repeat the proportions of the Tabernacle but on a larger scale. The placing of the Tabernacle in the western section also repeats the idea of the lowest part of a World being set within a larger area. Thus the Ark, which is the lower part of Emanation, is contained in the Holy of Holies or the upper part of Creation which, in turn, is contained in the lower part of Creation of the Sanctuary; which, again, is enveloped by the Tabernacle as a whole which is, in turn, surrounded by the Court where lower Formation is simultaneously the upper part of the World of Action. Beyond the fence of the Court lies the lower part of the Natural World which is subdivided into Levites and Israelites and all other nations under animal, vegetable and mineral law. Thus the scheme of the Worlds is complete.

The details of the outer wall clearly indicate the lower Worlds. To begin with, the metals used are silver and bronze. These represent Formation and Action. The fabric hung between the bronze posts is plain linen. It is only at the eastern end, where the gateway to the court stands, that panels of the four colours are used. Here five posts hold up four panels and so we get a repetition of the four levels and nine sefirot; the tenth always being considered out of vision in the levels above. The dimensions of one hundred cubits and fifty cubits may well symbolise the lower World interpenetrating half of its superior. Of all this we cannot be sure because the original text is undoubtedly incomplete and has certainly been modified; to illustrate the point, the last two verses of this chapter abruptly switch from the grand design into a minute sidetrack concerned with the ingredients for making lamp oil. This formula is probably priestcraft rather than an example of knowledge about the inner and upper Worlds.

Drawing away from the detail and viewing the Tabernacle in its setting at the centre of the Israelite camp, we see how it will become a focal point in the psychological and spiritual development of the people. Symbol of the inner and higher Worlds, the Tabernacle's presence will affect the tribes and influence them towards an ordered society based upon law founded in Divine principles. The erection of an inner Tabernacle within the individual by kabbalistic theory and practice creates and forms a similar centre of gravity which, in course of time, transforms the state of the psyche and spirit.

Seen in terms of Jacob's Ladder the Tabernacle articulates itself very accurately up through the various levels. At the bottom face of the physical Tree, the Israelites represent the activities and values of ordinary living. The Levites above represent a higher level of life

152

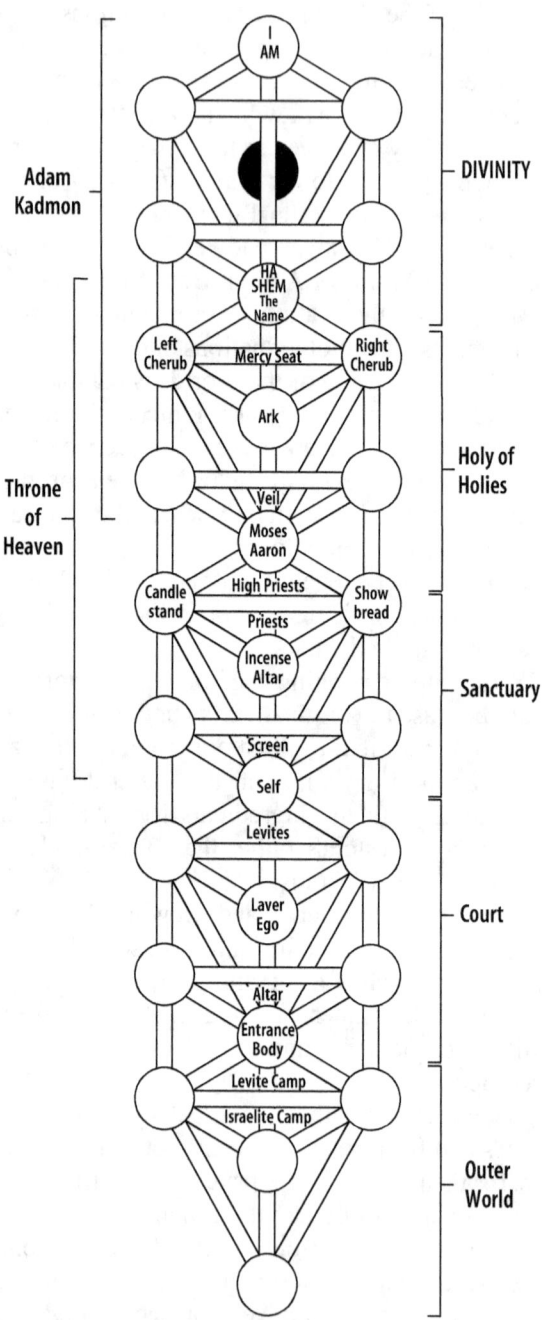

where standards are related to the Worlds above. The entrance to the Court and the triad of the Altar are the places where the physical translates into the Form of the lower psychological Tree, the Laver being the spot where the ego is cleansed (the Israelites were allowed into the court of upper Action). The door of the self to the Tent of Meeting is at the place where the three lower Worlds meet and the Soul triad acts as the screen before the sanctuary which separates the lower psyche from the face of the upper psychological and lower spiritual chambers of the sanctuary. Here, at the height of psychological Understanding and Wisdom are the Lamp standard and the Table of Showbread. The triad of spiritual Judgement and Mercy represents the inner veil before the Holy of Holies where the Ark sits at the place of spiritual Knowledge (just above the place where the three upper Worlds meet). Here between the Cherubim hovers *HaShem*, the Name of YAHVEH-ELOHIM, the God of Israel. Beyond the Abyss of Darkness is the Crown of I AM.

The emphasis of the scriptures now shifts away from the macrocosmic view embodied in the Tabernacle and concentrates on the microcosmic aspect of the Teaching related to man, as set out in the structure and rituals of the community.

Figure 34 (Left)—TABERNACLE LADDER
In this scheme the sacred objects represent different levels and rôles of the priesthood. The screen, for example, shields the entrance to the Sanctuary from those who have not yet reached a certain spiritual level. The reason for this is that Higher Knowledge gives power that can be misused by those who do not have wisdom and understanding. Only the High Priests were permitted to enter the Holy of Holies (Halevi, 20th century).

KNOWLEDGE OF MAN

HIGH PRIEST Esoteric Teaching upon the DIVINE in religion	**World of Emanation**
PRIESTS Mesoteric Teaching upon Spirit and Creation Cosmic Scheme in religion	**World of Creation**
LEVITES Exoteric Teaching upon soul Ethics and custom Psychological and social practice in religion	**World of Formation**
ISRAELITES Physical ritual in general and personal action Support upper levels Mundane work	**World of Action**

Figure 35 — HIERARCHY

These are the four levels of humanity. At the bottom are those at the vegetable level because they are, as yet, young souls. Above them come the Levites of animal rank who were the administrators of Israelite society. Beyond them are the priests at the human level of development while above them comes the High Priest who was supposed to be enlightened, at least while in the Holy of Holies. (Halevi, 20th century).

32. Human Hierarchy
EXODUS 28

As said, there is a clear differentiation between the House of Israel and the Children of Israel. The House of Israel refers to those who have access to the Creative World and come in direct contact with the Divine. Such people perceive Divine laws at work in the Worlds and in the individual. Known in other traditions as 'the wise', 'those who know' or 'the initiates', they are part of the interior circle of mankind which is concerned with the spiritual life of humanity.

In Exodus the division of the human race is symbolically set out according to the doctrine of the Four Worlds with the Children of Israel occupying the place of Action at the perimeter of the circles centred on the Holy of Holies.

At the top of this spiritual caste system are the High Priests. They belong to the Aaronite Clan and operate at the level of the Lower Divine, inasmuch as the High Priest can enter the Holy of Holies. The privilege of being the senior initiates, however, carries heavy duties and penalties if the role is abused. The death by wilful misadventure of two of Aaron's sons during the initiation of the Tabernacle is a warning to any who believe that there is nothing but advantage in being so exalted. This is emphasised in the provision to remove the body of the High Priest from the Holy of Holies should he die in there because of some sin that, in lesser men, might be considered trivial. The High Priesthood had to be an example of perfect integrity and purity in order to go safely into the Holiest of places. For this reason, they were not allowed to touch the dead, marry divorcées or come from a suspect pedigree in case of defilement. These and many other laws of the Priestly Code expressed the idea of fitness to enter into communion with the Divine. Because of this, only the High Priest's clan could hold and transmit the esoteric Teaching upon Divine matters.

The priests were those not of Aaron's immediate family. They corresponded to the level of Creation in that they served in the Holy sanctuary of the spirit. Their tasks were to assist the High Priests in the routine ceremonies and direct the other Levites in their work. One of the priests' tasks was to accompany the army as the religious presence in Israel's campaigns against unbelievers. Like the High Priests they were forbidden to do certain things that the two lower castes were allowed to do. This also was in order to preserve their spiritual integrity as they were responsible for teaching the mesoteric or cosmic aspects of the Torah. Israel's knowledge of the World of Creation was preserved by them over many centuries in certain families. Unfortunately, the tendency to hold such secrets close became exclusivity and so, according to spiritual law, it was taken from them and they were left with the shell of the Tradition. Providentially, the revelations of such prophets as Ezekiel and later mystics corrected this discrepancy for Israel and so the knowledge was retrieved and passed on into the rabbinical and Essene lines.

The Levites were the three clans of Merari, Gershon and Kohath. These were the representatives of Formation, the psychological level. Their task was not only to run the organisation of the Tabernacle but also to sing, play music and teach the exoteric Teaching on the Soul through social customs and practices. As the scribes of the nation, they were concerned with the cultural or psychological formation of the people. This was done by writing out, under higher direction, a history, based upon tribal saga and myth, intermixed with the Teaching. This was the beginning of the written tradition. Like the priests and High Priests, the Levites had no patrimony; that is, they had no physical inheritance. This was not only because the Lord was said to be their legacy but because, as symbols of the psyche, they could only possess a token connection with the physical World—as expressed in the Levite cities to be granted to them when Israel entered Canaan. In the Tabernacle complex, the Levites served principally in the court where they acted as intermediaries between the priesthood and the Israelites who were allowed to enter the outer gate in order to participate in the worship.

The Israelites were the vast majority of the nation and represented the ordinary level of being born, maturing, marrying, bearing children, ageing and dying. Here, in the outer and lower World of Action, physical laws had their maximum effect. The Levites and the priests were protected from these problems by the people who fed and clothed them and bore the brunt of attacks from enemies, both physical and psychological, who assaulted the outer perimeter of the camp with violence or tried to seduce or draw out the Israelites by customs that appealed to the senses and lower psyche. Ego-oriented, easily influenced, seeking to avoid pain and find pleasure, the Israelites symbolise the psyche still largely subject to the World of Nature with its elemental moods and tooth-and-claw values. Without the presence of the other three levels, the Israelites would soon have been defeated or demoralised or broken up into internal tribal factions. This would have led most certainly to dissolution and absorption into the polytheistic cults surrounding them. On the individual level this is a picture of the natural human condition without an awareness of the soul, the guidance of the Spirit and the Grace of the Divine as expressed in the Levites, priests and High Priest.

Taking the role of the High Priest as the symbol of the perfect man, let us examine Exodus 28 to see how the design of the vestments follows the doctrine of the four levels as the idealised image of an evolved human being.

33. Levels in Man
Exodus 28

'Veaseetah vigedai kodesh' 'And thou shalt make Holy garment for Aaron thy brother', *'LeKavod oole Tiferet'* 'for the Glory and for the Beauty. And thou shalt speak unto all the wise-hearted whom I have refined with the *Ruah Hokhmah* 'Spirit of Wisdom' (Exodus 28:2-3). The text then goes on to set out the general scheme of the garments. These are a breast-plate and ephod, a mantle, a chequered coat, a turban and a girdle. Later a pair of breeches is added, making seven elements in all. This number in itself indicates the seven levels or stations of consciousness but at this point we will limit ourselves to the four Worlds.

The ephod or over-raiment is the first garment to be specified in detail. Sewn into a coat of linen are to be strands of gold, blue, purple and scarlet yarn. The gold signifies the Divine spark in man, the blue thread his spiritual vehicle, the purple his psychological organism and the scarlet the colour of blood for the physical body. This richly embroidered garment was held at the shoulders by two straps while affixed to its front was a breast-plate of gold, inset with twelve precious stones arranged in four rows of three. This breast-plate was held by two chains of gold to a pair of carnelian stones, one on each shoulder, set in two golden rosettes. The cornelians were engraved with the names of the sons of Israel, six on one side and six on the other. These matched the stones of the breast-plate in that each stone was related to one of the tribes. The lower part of the breast-plate was secured by blue threads to the ephod.

The original meaning, like the translation of the words *ephod* and *hoshen* for the breast-plate, has been lost with time, so there has been much speculation about the stones, their names and arrangement. Some rabbis see the order of fraternal seniority as a progression from right to left, indicating a Lightning Flash-like descent of Divine principles, while others view the breast-plate lay-out as the sefirotic Tree with the addition of the three *Zahzahot* or Hidden Splendours of later Kabbalah that precede the sefirot; the Crown being simultaneously a link between the Tree and the concealed roots of the pillars. Many rabbis saw the letters of the names of the tribes as making up the many Names of God, in particular the *Shem Ha Meforash* or the Special Name of the Lord. This title only the High Priests knew how to verbalise and utter before the people on the highest Holy Day of Atonement.

According to legend, the brightness of the stones was used for oracular purposes. Thus, when an important question had to be asked it was addressed to the High Priest in his full regalia. The Breast-plate, folklore relates, then responded by lighting up certain of the stones and letters of the alphabet; thus words would be formed into an answer. Whatever this method may have actually symbolised, the Breast-plate was considered infallible, provided the High Priest had sufficient purity of heart and intellectual clarity, that is, psychological balance and developed spirit.

Behind the ephod was the pouch of the *Urim* and *Thummim*. What they actually were has been lost, although it is known that they were also used for oracular purposes. According to some, a question was asked and, depending on whether the Urim or Thummim was drawn out, the answer was determined aye or nay. These methods of divination were used when there was an important issue confronting the nation. Their operation was exclusively in the hands of the High Priest which guarded against an oracle of a lower angelic or even demonic order from taking precedence over the Divine.

The Breast-plate and the Urim and Thummim represent the lower part of the Divine World. Later in the text, the upper part of Emanation is symbolised by a turban and a plate made of pure gold with the words *Kodosh le YAHVEH* or 'Holy to YAHVEH' engraved upon it. This Holy Name represents the Crown of the Tree of Creation which is at the centre of the Divine World. Thus Aaron wears, over his head and heart, the symbols and the instrument whereby the High Priest may know the Divine Will.

The mantle of blue with its sky colour not only represents the Creative World but the spiritual organism within a human being. The pomegranates hung round its skirts were symbols of the potency of Creation while the bells hung between them were to make a sound that could be heard outside the Holy of Holies. This music told those outside that the High Priest was still living in the flesh as he moved in the protecting darkness before the Shekhinah's radiance that hovered over the Ark. The significance of this for the individual is that the spirit is contained by the Divine and underlies it, just as the heavenly throne is placed below the Glory in Ezekiel's vision. The celestial colour of the garment indicates the universal scale of this spiritual level where the body vanishes and the psyche is reduced to a dot. Only those who can function in the cosmic state of consciousness may approach and enter the Holy of Holies safely.

The chequered coat represents the psychological body, the squares indicating the interaction of opposites and the subsequent combinations of attraction, repulsion and equilibrium experienced in the ever-changing situation of the psychological World of Formation. The chequers also reveal how the Soul has to choose constantly between good and evil as circumstance continually alters in fluctuation as Heaven above undergoes the travail of Creation and influences the Worlds below. This garment worn below the two upper coats is the longest and reaches to the ground. It is in contact with the physical body of the priest on its inner side and acts as an insulator from, and connection with, the blue coat just as the psyche does between the body and the spirit. There is probably a touch of contact with the Ephod at its top to establish a Divine connection, as indicated on Jacob's Ladder.

A sash made up of the three sacred colours is wound round the waist and so each coat is separated into its superior and inferior level thus signifying, with the varying lengths of the coats, the interleaving of the Worlds and bodies. The breeches of linen worn to cover the genitals during the time in the Holy place indicate a mystery of Yesod, the sefirah of the Foundation, which springs from the unmanifest sefirah of Knowledge (Daat) at a higher level. The implied meaning of this is that nothing secret should be revealed to the inferior levels. The Hebrew name for Foundation is Yesod which contains an inner word, Sod, which means secret.

For the individual, the description of the vestments of the High Priest is an account of his own composition. Here are the four levels of his being set out as they truly are. The Divine is not only at his centre but encloses the spirit or cosmic aspect of himself within which, in turn, his psyche resides and contains the nucleus of the physical body. This is the esoteric principle of 'As above so below' at work in Biblical terms. In the undeveloped the three lower vehicles, the chariots as they are sometimes called, are in various stages of evolution. The physical body is perhaps the most evolved in sophistication with the psychological organism, in many people, in a state of gestation or early development.

The spiritual anatomy in most individuals is probably an amorphous cloud; but the Divine part is, like the exquisitely woven Ephod, already perfect.

34. Degeneration of Knowledge
EXODUS 29

If the Tabernacle represents the Creative World of the Universe and the vestments of the priests the bodies of man, the rituals specified on the Mountain relate to the unification of the two. Here, however, we have to remember that the scriptures may have been modified by the Priestly Code inserted during or after the first Exile to Babylon (circa sixth century BCE) which has many elements of priestcraft. To perceive this, one must examine the text with a critical eye and not believe that everything in the Bible is only Holy Writ. Such a view is usually held by those without esoteric knowledge or a grasp of the historical background of the scriptures. The Bible was certainly inspired by God; but human beings who possessed different levels of comprehension translated what they understood and this, in turn, has been altered by scribes and copyists who have diluted, omitted and even added certain texts. The result is that the written canon is only, the rabbis agree, a fragment of its original content.

An example of this phenomenon is witnessed in the twenty-ninth chapter of Exodus. Some portions of it are based upon Moses's revelation but the rest is probably the addition of a scribe who is more preoccupied with the elaborate ceremony than its meaning. Blood sacrifice may well have been the authentic ritual form at that time but the pre-occupation with details like the long lobe of the liver, and what to do with the kidneys, clearly has more connection with priestcraft than with higher knowledge. An experience of spiritual reality, some psychological common sense and a little scholarship soon begin to separate out what is authentic.

In the opening verses, a young bull and two rams without blemish are to be brought forward at the beginning of the consecration of Aaron and his sons. So, too, are unleavened loaves, cakes and wafers, all mixed or smeared with oil. Here we have the animal and vegetable kingdoms. Then the initiates are to be ushered into the court of the Tabernacle, that is out of the outer physical World into the lower psychological level. There they stand before the entrance to the Tent where the three lower Worlds meet. Here they are washed at the Laver or the ego position. Aaron is then dressed in the sequence of vestments, beginning with the under-garments and finishing with the turban and plate of Holy Dedication on the head. This investiture is symbolic of the evolutionary process of the body, Soul and Spirit. The anointing with oil represents the Divine Grace coming down over Aaron's Crown. The same sequence of initiation is then to be applied to his sons.

The rank of priest is said in the text to be held for ever but here we must recall that many priests abused their position, so that the priestly caste was eventually to lose the respect of the people through its corrupt ways and interest in worldly power. With the destruction of the second Temple by the Romans their influence was reduced to a token. This raises the question: who is the author of the words, 'And the priests' office shall be theirs for a perpetual statute' in Exodus 29:9? Was it a Divine instruction or a priest protecting his privilege?

Next in the text comes the slaughter of the bull and the consecration of the altar with its blood, after which comes the burning of the fat, liver and kidneys. The skin and offal are to be destroyed outside the camp. This raises the question: why is the death of the animal necessary? Besides its functions as a food offering to the Deity, the ancients believed that a ritual killing heightened the senses, as the release of the vitality of the sacrifice affected those present at the moment of death. This phenomenon was used to raise the level of the celebrants so as to perceive a glimpse into the next World, as many present at a death have experienced. The choice of a bull was because it was the epitome of physical power and abundance. It was also seen as a symbol of what is to be given up in order to obtain access to the higher Worlds and states. The organs burnt at the altar represented the trans-substantiation of earthly materiality into a subtler anatomy. The burning of the skin and offal outside the camp is the recognition in ritual that not all that is offered can be transmuted because it is of the outer or lower World. Therefore it is taken out of the court and camp to be returned to the elemental realms of Earth.

The two rams were then to be slaughtered. The first was another burnt food offering to placate the Deity while the second ram's blood was put on the right ears, thumbs and toes of Aaron and his sons before it also was flung against the altar. This again is probably the description of a symbolic ceremony that had become corrupted by priests who no longer knew anything more than the outer form. The text goes on to describe how the ram's blood should be sprinkled over Aaron's and his sons' vestments, that they might become holy. This is an account of an event that at one time must have had much more to it than what is described, if its purpose was really to make a man and his garments become holy. These rituals are forms of high magic in that the physical performance of certain actions evokes the occult powers of the psychological World. However magic, or the art of manipulating the World of Formation, no matter how efficacious, is not of the same order as the miraculous which is the spiritual power of the World of Creation. Magic, as pointed out earlier, is of an inferior order because it has only one contact, at the very Crown of Formation, with the Divine; and this connection most magicians avoid because they want only to exercise their own will. That is why magic was fiercely discouraged in Israel.

The rest of the chapter is mostly concerned with the detailing of the rituals. It describes what is to be done with the rams' innards and right leg, the breast and the head; and how that which is not burnt as a food offering shall belong to Aaron and his sons. Here, again, an objective eye must consider the element of self-interest that was to creep into priestly conduct over the centuries. Time was to prove again and again that they were subject to mortal rather than spiritual motivations.

After a seven-day initiation of the priestly caste, the text moves on to the more routine sacrifices. Here are described the creatures and objects to be used and at what times of day they should be offered. A precise recipe, for example, for one sacrifice is set down in verses 39 and 40. The literary effect is closer to a badly edited instruction manual than a document of Divine revelation. It is only in the last verse of the chapter that revelation once again breaks forth in the promise that God will meet Moses at the Tabernacle after it has been sanctified and Aaron and his sons have been consecrated. The words, 'And I will dwell among the Children of Israel and be their God', raise the whole level out of the trivial. The final verse, 'And they shall know that I AM YAHVEH-ELOHIM', takes the text right up to its original quality. Here is a most useful exercise, for an individual must learn to recognise the difference between levels in his studies and have the integrity to act upon conclusions based on personal experience, not hearsay, however reputable.

35. Regeneration of Knowledge
Exodus 30-31

The opening verses of Exodus chapter 30 lay out the specification of the altar for incense to be set before the veil of the Holy of Holies in the sanctuary. It is to be made of shittim wood and overlaid with pure gold, including the horns and carrying poles. In it Aaron is to burn incense morning and evening. On it shall be put only authorised incense and Aaron shall put blood on its horns once a year for atonement. Here we have, again, a mixture of esoteric instruction and priestcraft. The incense altar, it should be noted, is almost an afterthought, quite separate from the initial directions on the sacred furniture and the Tabernacle. Perhaps the priests were copying local custom or even adapting the burner so as to conform to standard practice.

The use of incense is not only to send a pleasing aroma up to the Deity but to put the priests and assembly into a heightened state. This bio-chemical technique is a universally recognised method of raising the consciousness. Unfortunately, such drug-induced states without any inner training merely bring about a slight separation between the body and the psyche and so precipitate a sense of distorted reality which often brings forth not only strange visions but any imbalance within the psyche. Under the regime of a skilled teacher, such aberrations can be safeguarded against by rigid discipline and codes of purity. Nevertheless, the practice of inhaling incense carries its hazards and may be regarded as an artificial way of ascension into the upper Worlds.

An indication of an interpolated text or omission of some crucial lead-in passage comes in the eleventh verse. Here the Israelites are to be registered and the financial arrangements for a man's ransom to the Lord are specified. Now, while it is right to be beholden to the Creator for one's life, the way the text presents it approaches extortion. Perhaps some priests drafted these verses, not without some self-interest. The text states how many shekels should be given as a contribution to the Lord and how the rich and poor have to pay the same. This appears to be contrary to natural or Divine Justice. The paragraph finishes this rule by saying that the money shall be an atonement for their souls as well as towards the upkeep of the Tabernacle. Here is a highly suspect justification for supporting the clergy. It is the acquisition of wealth and power by playing upon the fear and guilt of the unlearned. A severe comment, perhaps, but alas a phenomenon commonly witnessed in all religious establishments throughout the world.

The text at Exodus 30:17 switches back to the making of the bronze laver. This, once more, reveals inconsistent editing on some scribe's part. The washing of the hands and feet of the priests is described before they enter the Tent of the Presence 'lest they die'—from impurity. This might be a prod at the priesthood that they may be far from faultless.

Exodus 30:22 then focuses right down to a list of materials for making the anointing oil and its application to the Tabernacle and each object and piece of furniture within it. This is symbolic of the Dew of Heaven gracing the Place of Meeting. After saying how Aaron and his sons must be anointed and that the oil must be used for nothing else, the scribe ends the chapter with a most detailed list of spices and how to make them into incense for the altar. Here esoteric knowledge has turned into simple information.

As if in reaction and contrast to the foregoing, the text again completely changes its character by introducing the name of a man called Bezalel which means 'in the shadow of God' (the son of Hur who helped Moses in the battle with the Amalekites). This Israelite, the Lord explains to Moses, has been filled with the Spirit of the Divine *Be Hokhmah uvitevunah* 'in Wisdom and Understanding', *uveDaat* 'and in Knowledge'. Here we observe the upper sefirot of the Tree. Bezalel is to be the builder of the Tabernacle 'in all manner of skills'. His assistant is to be Aholiab which means 'the Tent of his Father'. In Jewish folklore he is not only called Bezalel 'the shadow of God' but also Reaiah which means 'to behold for he was a man who was seen by God'. He was also called Jahath, 'the Trembler', because he has experienced awe of the Divine and 'the one who unified' because his work brought about the connection between God and Israel.

Sometimes Kabbalah is called the Work of Unification and in this knowledge we are informed that Bezalel exceeded even Moses at times. He knew, for example, the correct shape and specifications of the Lamp standard without being told by Moses who had forgotten them even though he had been shown the design twice on the Mountain. According to tradition, Bezalel also knew how to combine the twenty-two letters of the Hebrew alphabet that went to bring about Creation. Seen kabbalistically, this means that Bezalel was a man who had practice as well as theory of the Creative World. This is why he was given the task of carrying out the designs given to Moses.

These fragments from the Oral Law give us some insight concerning the Elders of Israel who were privy to the Teaching. They had a role quite separate from the priesthood and constituted the inner aspect of the spiritual line. On the Tree of the Community they occupied the right, Force, pillar of prophecy with Moses that complemented the left, Form, pillar of Aaron and the priesthood.

Seen in the individual, Bezalel represents that aspect of a person which corresponds with the creative self. At the focus of Wisdom, Understanding and Knowledge, the self is the individuality that reflects the Creator. Operating like most artists, Bezalel knows what to do intuitively as he receives the Grace descending from Knowledge. Thus the sefirah of Beauty can construct the Tabernacle within the being of the person. This unification of the Worlds in the self slowly produces sacred object after sacred object until the Sanctuary and its Court is realised above and below. In time, the inner Tabernacle becomes the place of meeting between the Divine and man. Here begins, at the individual level, the initial stage of the process whereby I and Thou face each other and God begins to behold God. The name Bezalel, which is also interpreted as 'Beholding the Deity if only in shadow', reflects this principle.

36. Day of Recreation
EXODUS 31

In the last phase of Moses's instruction on the Mountain the Lord speaks of the Sabbath. The day is to symbolise the original Sabbath when God rested from the Work of bringing the World of Creation into being. It, however, contains much else.

The scripture says, 'Above all you shall observe My sabbaths, for the sabbath is a sign between Me and you in every generation that you may know that I AM the LORD who hallows you'. This statement not only commands a recognition of the cycle of Creation but makes it a weekly memorial wherein the Israelites acknowledge their Creator. The significance of this commandment was to be borne out in later days when the Temple was destroyed and there was no longer any physical Tabernacle, for the Sabbath was still celebrated even in the most difficult times all over the world. If anything kept the people of Israel in touch with their destiny it was the observation of this commandment.

The Sabbath is a day of rest. It comes at the end of a cycle related to the four phases of the Moon; thus there is embodied in this rhythm an acknowledgement of the interaction of Heaven and Earth. The plant and animal kingdoms live within this daily and monthly rhythm as they progress through the Solar year. Mankind, which contains a vegetable and animal level within its being, also has to submit to these cycles. The Sabbath at this level provides rest, recreation and a pause in the working cycle for time to reflect upon the greater Worlds and their Creator, as well as a stop to look inwardly at the interior universe of the Spirit. It is often only during such periods of regulated quiet that we perceive things outside our own little realm of ego and its immediate circle.

Work was forbidden on this day because 'It is Holy to you', that is, it is set aside for the purpose of seeing the 'whole' which has the same Old English root meaning as Holy. Totality is quite a different scale from anything less. That is why the scripture goes on to say that 'Those profaning it shall surely be put to death' in a rabbinical translation meaning 'If you break cosmic law it can kill you'. The word is not 'must' or 'will' but 'surely' which changes it into a speculative proposition because as the text continues 'for everyone that works on it [the Sabbath] that soul shall be cut off from the midst of his people'. This means that the connection between the body, soul and Spirit will be lost and the unity of the being and his development impaired, if not damaged permanently. Anyone who has worked excessive hours knows the self-estranged state where the body and mind, let alone the soul and Spirit, are disoriented. The warning of being cut off is not a threat but profound observation about those who disregard the cycle of Creation and lose themselves in overwork and reflectionless activity. It should be remembered at this point that on the day prior to the Sabbath a double portion of manna always fell, half the manna keeping until the seventh day. In this symbol is the law that Providence takes care of anyone observing it. Indeed this is true for anybody who turns his attention to higher things and seeks the Kingdom of Heaven, that is, in Kabbalah, the spiritual level of the self. Then, as a later great Jewish mystic said, 'All else will be added unto you'.

On the social level the Sabbath was when the family were together. Wearing their clean and finest clothes, they would celebrate the wedding of the Sabbath which was seen as a Bride in the union of Heaven and Earth. This marriage was symbolised by the weekly conjugal act between a man and his wife on the eve of the Sabbath. Kabbalah saw such a union as an aid in the unification of the upper and lower Worlds because, in Judaic tradition, esoteric work was not designed to escape the mundane but to bring the soul and Spirit into contact with the body so as to enhance the Earth with the upper Worlds. Thus the Sabbath union of Adam and Eve brought right and left Pillars and above and below together as face gazed upon face in the microcosmos of a human relationship. This is why sexual symbolism is used in Kabbalistic literature.

According to the rabbis, those who observe the Sabbath acquire an extra soul. By this is meant that to the body, psyche and Spirit is added a fourth level called *Hayyah*, that is, Divine consciousness. This state is said to last throughout the Sabbath and give to the person an experience of Grace. At the end of the day the Hayyah is withdrawn and the person reverts to his normal state. For the individual who is working on his inner development, the Sabbath is clearly an extra-special day in that, with the Hayyah's aid, his body, psyche and Spirit can be more easily receptive to the Divinity within. By nightfall, if only for a few hours longer, he may be able to retain contact with the Hayyah.

Traditionally, the Sabbath is devoted to worship and study. Generally a portion of the Torah is read in the synagogue and a sermon is given. This keeps the Teaching before the people with the sermon relating to current problems that confront the community and individual. According to custom, the afternoon is spent studying the commentary of the sages on the week's scriptural passage. The degree of comprehension depends on the stage of development of both the teacher and instructed. Thus, while one school might be preoccupied with a fine legal point, another group might well be concerned with the esoteric meaning of that same text. This way of spending the Sabbath has been observed from generation to generation over many centuries.

While the outer or exoteric rules, practices and customs were refined into a code regarding the Sabbath, esoteric work brought a rich mystery into the day of rest. For example, the Sabbath was seen as the Malkhut or Kingdom of the week containing all the days that had gone before. The Sabbath was also perceived as the turning-point back towards the Crown of the New Moon as it waxed and waned through the four weeks or Worlds of the month. The Sabbath was considered to be in many ways as important as, if not more important than, the High Holy Days because it had been commanded on Mount Sinai.

When God had finished instructing Moses upon the Sabbath he was given the two stone Tablets of Testimony and sent down into the lower Worlds, having been upon the mountain for forty days and nights. During this time much had also happened amongst the Israelites as they waited with increasing impatience, flagging will and fading discipline for his return. It is at such crucial moments, at the high point of initiation, that the individual is tested, not in his strongest area but where the demons of chaos can gain the easiest access.

Revolt

Figure 36 — REGRESSION

When Moses came down from Mount Sinai he found that some Israelites had regressed and were worshipping the idol of a bull, a symbol of physicality and sensuality. He was so angry that he broke the Tablets of the Teaching because he believed the Israelites were not worthy to be taught. This kind of backsliding can occur when a teacher is not present. Fortunately the Levites remained loyal to Moses. They are the equivalent of conscience in the individual. (Rev.T. Bankes's Bible, 19th century).

37. Defection
Exodus 32

The first verse of Exodus chapter 32 opens with the words, 'And when the people saw that Moses delayed to come down out of the mount the people gathered themselves unto Aaron and said unto him, "Rise up, make us a god, which shall go before us"'.

According to the folklore that runs parallel to the scriptures, the trouble began among the mixed multitude that had come out of Egypt with the Israelites. These consisted of a variety of people who, for various reasons, wanted to leave that state of life and seek another. The promise of freedom had great appeal and many Egyptians left their country with the Israelites to escape from the past or find some new kind of future. After three months in the desert the initial enthusiasm and novelty had worn off; while the Israelites at least had some sort of common aim to return to the land promised them, the mixed multitude of inferior habits and motivations tried to re-create Egypt in the desert. During Moses's absence the leadership of the people was in the hands of an as-yet uninitiated Aaron and a collection of good but inexperienced Elders. The mixed multitude, perceiving weakness in the temporary rulers, began to turn the now restless Israelites aside from their covenant at the very moment of its reception. While most Israelites knew that all that was required of them was to wait, a few could not endure the inaction with patience. This trial is often the most hard for many individuals about to take up a spiritual commitment. Having given their word, they believe they are ready to take on anything and everything. When nothing happens for a long time, the depth of their verbal covenant is revealed and their ability to maintain direction during periods of waiting without guidance is tested.

In Jewish legend Satan the tester, with Jannes and Jambres, two students of Balaam the magician, conjure up before the increasingly disturbed and doubting children of Israel the image of a dead Moses floating on a bier midway between Heaven and Earth. This symbolism displays the scribes' knowledge of the Worlds. The precise location and height of the bier defines, to those who know even a little kabbalistic theory, that Jannes and Jambres were working in the World of Formation that lies between the Worlds of Action and Creation. When the Israelites saw the mirage they fell into despair: if their leader had gone, what would become of them in the desert between Egypt and Canaan? Satan, taking full advantage of the situation, worked on the growing disorder among the tribes. Months of work were undermined in days and the half-completed initiation of Sinai was to become more than just threatened. Seeing no sign of Moses or God, Satan openly tempted the strained and now shocked Israelites. In the individual, such satanic attack comes when exhaustion weakens resolution and only a sharp but subtle push is needed to throw the aspirant off the spiritual path. The magicians represent the inner tricksters of mischief and fantasy who plague all spiritual exercises.

It was at this point that the mixed multitude, exerting their influence as the only cohesive group, began to pressure Aaron and the Elders. The two sorcerers, who considered Moses only a rival magician, utilised this force to direct the people's attention to worshipping the gods of the World of Formation. Hur, the man who had stood by Moses in the battle against the Amalekites, stepped forward and rebuked the people for their ingratitude to God who had done so much for them. He was instantly killed by a now violently aroused collection of the mixed multitude and some Israelites who had been infected by the excitement. Having so easily disposed of one leader, the mob then turned upon Aaron, clamouring, 'make us a god or we will slay thee also'. Aaron, we are told, becoming less concerned with his own life than with preventing the rot going further, sought to stall them when he consented to make a god. In order to gain time so that the people might cool down, he issued instructions for the collection of personal golden ornaments. This ploy, Aaron hoped, would make them think twice before making the idol.

The meaning of this for the individual is that during such a revolt against a spiritual discipline, an instructor will try to offset rapid disintegration by various holding actions until the person comes to his senses. In this situation an individual might be promised some privilege on condition that it is paid for by giving something in return. This follows the law that everything, good or evil, has to be paid for sooner or later. The fee for what is to be done is often too expensive for the ego and frequently stops the destructive process. In our legend, Aaron's device slowed the revolt down but did not stop it, so powerful was the flow of dissipating energy. Legend goes on to tell how the menfolk at first sought to take their women's jewellery so as to avoid personal cost; but this was refused and so the men reluctantly gave their own vanities to Aaron. This bought time but not enough; for Moses was still upon the Mountain.

When the golden ornaments brought from Egypt were thrown into the melting pit they fused spontaneously into a bull calf. There are various traditional explanations for this. The Bull, besides being the symbol of animal vitality, is one of the four Holy Animals that appear in the Bible and symbolises the World of the Earth and Action. However, here the image of a Calf indicates not only immaturity but the lack of any contact with the Divine World of Emanation. As a physical representation for the bodily senses to worship, it reveals a spiritual regression. Another interpretation is that when Israel had crossed the Red Sea, some Israelites had sensed the Divine presence on the Throne-Chariot drawn by the four Holy Creatures above them. However, only the Bull of the Physical World was perceived and therefore the Israelites concluded that it must be the God that brought them out of Egypt. For an individual this is the equivalent of considering a physical teacher, symbol or Tradition as Divinity itself. The commandment, 'No other gods before Me', safeguards against this tendency in early spiritual work.

Legend tells us that when the Golden Calf appeared it spontaneously took on life. Symbolically, this is because the people's combined will and need projected vitality into it and so it lived for them. Here is a common group phenomenon. It is observed that such gods, be they individuals or organisations, take on a charismatic role or life of their own by feeding upon the psychic vitality given to them. The people, seeing their idol or externalised mass ego infused with such great power, demanded that the Elders recognise it as their god. Several Elders openly opposed this ignorant view and were killed. The twelve prince-leaders of the Tribes, seeing the fate of those who denied the will of the multitude, joined the surviving Elders and did not answer the summons of the mob who wished to confront them. Retreat is sometimes the only option available to a teacher with a disaffected student. Confrontation only increases the ego's sense of itself. The multitude taking it that all authority was vanquished (the most common Aunt Sally of spiritual rebellion) then proceeded to celebrate the victory by having an orgy round their idol. Most Israelites were confused or frightened by these events and many were drawn into the celebrations either by a wilful reaction to the strict discipline of Moses or by will-less acceptance of what was happening. In the course of a few days the whole camp became affected so that the attention focused on what was going on at the top of the Mountain was forgotten. Such a situation is not unknown to those who, having thrown discipline away, release an accumulated reservoir of psychological energy in an orgy of extremely violent acts of self-destruction. Legend says that a virulent illness struck the camp which, like the mad and disordered growth of cancer, penetrated deep into the body and psyche of the Israelites. If it were not cut out in time, then all Israel would be destroyed.

38. Inner Conflict
EXODUS 32

In terms of the individual, the episode of the Golden Calf represents a crisis of the greatest magnitude. Just as the maximum contact with the Divine is made, so the maximum resistance is met from the psyche which throws the whole being into disarray. The entire initiation is placed in jeopardy. This is a major point of breakthrough or breakdown of spiritual work for, when the full implication of commitment is realised, the true intention and motivation of an individual is tested. Such moments are used by Satan, the dark side of the psyche, to exploit weaknesses and so destroy any unity of being that has been acquired. Doubt, reasoned argument, irrational fears are brought into violent confrontation with faith, knowledge and courage as advancing and resisting factions struggle within the psyche. The wilder elements disturb the unconscious and panic the psyche's Foundation which becomes a rallying point for every dissident thought, feeling and action as the ego, realising it is about to lose its dominant role, puffs itself up to the enormous proportions of a god. This is the Golden Calf which is set up in order to compete with and defeat something deep within the psyche that the ego cannot comprehend.

In the scripture Aaron says to the people dancing round the idol, 'This is the god that brought you up out of Egypt?' It is a rhetorical question in the Jewish style. (In modern idiom, 'you must be joking'.) At this point Moses, high up on the Mountain, is informed by the Divine, 'Get thee down for thy people ... have corrupted themselves. They have turned aside quickly from the Way which I commanded them'. There is a long pause implied by the translation in the New English Bible, 'I have considered this people and I see they are stubborn', meaning rigid, fixed and unable to change from their old ways. From here on the severe side of the Deity manifests in the words, 'Now therefore let Me alone that My wrath may wax hot against them and that I may consume them'. At first sight it seems that the situation had gone too far to remedy. The text suggests that it would be better to

בְּרֵאשִׁ֖ית
GENESIS.
CHAPTER I. א

Let-[there]-be	יְהִ֥י	1. In-[the]-beginning	בְּרֵאשִׁ֖ית
[an]-expanse	רָקִ֖יעַ	²God ¹created	בָּרָ֣א אֱלֹהִ֑ים
in-the-midst-of the-waters,	בְּת֣וֹךְ הַמָּ֑יִם	a) ( )the-heaven	אֵ֥ת הַשָּׁמַ֖יִם
and-let-it divide	וִיהִ֣י מַבְדִּ֔יל	and-( ) the-earth.	וְאֵ֥ת הָאָֽרֶץ׃
between waters e) and-waters.	בֵּ֥ין מַ֖יִם לָמָֽיִם׃	2. And-the-earth	2· וְהָאָ֗רֶץ
7. ¹And ²God ¹made	7· וַיַּ֣עַשׂ אֱלֹהִים֮	was	הָיְתָ֥ה
( ) the-expanse	אֶת־הָרָקִיעַ֒	b) [a] desolation	תֹ֙הוּ֙
and-divided	וַיַּבְדֵּ֗ל	and c) [a] waste,	וָבֹ֔הוּ
between the-waters	בֵּ֤ין הַמַּ֙יִם֙	and-darkness [was]	וְחֹ֖שֶׁךְ
which [were] f) under d)the-expanse	אֲשֶׁר֙ מִתַּ֣חַת לָרָקִ֔יעַ	upon-the-face-of [the] abyss	עַל־פְּנֵ֣י תְה֑וֹם
and-(between) the-waters	וּבֵ֣ין הַמַּ֔יִם	and-the-spirit-of God	וְר֣וּחַ אֱלֹהִ֔ים
which [were] g) above d) the-expanse,	אֲשֶׁ֖ר מֵעַ֣ל לָרָקִ֑יעַ	moved	מְרַחֶ֖פֶת
and-it-was so.	וַֽיְהִי־כֵֽן׃	upon-the-face-of the-waters.	עַל־פְּנֵ֥י הַמָּֽיִם׃
8. ¹And ²God ¹called	8· וַיִּקְרָ֧א אֱלֹהִ֛ים	3. ¹And ²God ¹said:	3· וַיֹּ֥אמֶר אֱלֹהִ֖ים
d) the-expanse	לָֽרָקִ֖יעַ	Let-there-be light;	יְהִ֣י א֑וֹר
Heaven.	שָׁמָ֑יִם	and-there-was light.	וַֽיְהִי־אֽוֹר׃
And-it-was evening	וַיְהִי־עֶ֥רֶב	4. ¹And ²God ¹saw	4· וַיַּ֧רְא אֱלֹהִ֛ים
and-it-was morning,	וַיְהִי־בֹ֖קֶר	( ) the-light	אֶת־הָא֖וֹר
[a] ²second ¹day.	י֥וֹם שֵׁנִֽי׃	that [it was] good;	כִּי־ט֑וֹב
9. ¹And ²God ¹said:	9· וַיֹּ֣אמֶר אֱלֹהִ֗ים	¹and ²God ¹divided	וַיַּבְדֵּ֣ל אֱלֹהִ֔ים
'Let ²the-waters ¹be h) collected	יִקָּו֨וּ הַמַּ֜יִם	between the light	בֵּ֥ין הָא֖וֹר
f) under the-heaven	מִתַּ֤חַת הַשָּׁמַ֙יִם֙	and-(between) the-darkness.	וּבֵ֥ין הַחֹֽשֶׁךְ׃
unto ³one ²place,	אֶל־מָק֣וֹם אֶחָ֔ד	5. ¹And ²God ¹called	5· וַיִּקְרָ֨א אֱלֹהִ֤ים
¹and-let ²the dry-[land] i) ¹be-seen.	וְתֵרָאֶ֖ה הַיַּבָּשָׁ֑ה	d) the-light	לָאוֹר֙
and-it-was so.	וַֽיְהִי־כֵֽן׃	Day,	י֔וֹם
10. ¹And ²God ¹called	10· וַיִּקְרָ֨א אֱלֹהִ֤ים	and- d) the-darkness	וְלַחֹ֖שֶׁךְ
d) the-dry-[land]	לַיַּבָּשָׁה֙	he-called	קָ֣רָא
Earth;	אֶ֔רֶץ	Night.	לָ֑יְלָה
and- d) the-collection-of-the-waters	וּלְמִקְוֵ֥ה הַמַּ֖יִם	And-it-was evening,	וַֽיְהִי־עֶ֥רֶב
he-called Seas;	קָרָ֣א יַמִּ֑ים	and-it-was morning,	וַֽיְהִי־בֹ֖קֶר
¹and ²God ¹saw	וַיַּ֥רְא אֱלֹהִ֖ים	²one ¹day.	י֥וֹם אֶחָֽד׃
that [it was] good.	כִּי־טֽוֹב׃	6. ¹And ²God ¹said:	6· וַיֹּ֣אמֶר אֱלֹהִ֗ים

Figure 37 — THE PENTATEUCH

The Bible was to be crucial in the generation of the three monotheistic religions. The stories, symbols and instruction given in the context of Jewish history were recognisable in terms of everyday reality. People could identify with its characters, family problems and political situations. This enabled them to receive the Teaching about morality, the universe and the Almighty in terms they could understand. (Magil's Linear Bible).

dissolve the whole operation, destroy the corruption and begin again, even as death is sometimes the only way out of an impossible situation. This is implied in an offer to Moses who represents the most evolved part of Israel; that is, that which survives physical death and reappears in a new birth. God says to Moses, 'And I will make thee a great nation'. This was said also to Abraham, indicating a completely new line. However, the anger and despair of God, according to folklore, is a charade because the Divine had already anticipated the defection of the people. The event was an important lesson to show what happens when a nation or person steps off the spiritual way. The offer was made to Moses to see how he reacted. Such tests are not unknown among human mentors to prove the integrity of a disciple. A contrived situation, in which an appeal is made to the student's vanity, can sometimes reveal a vainglory of spirit that is infinitely more dangerous than any psychological pride or physical arrogance.

However, Moses reminded God of the promise given to the patriarchs, as he, legend records, noticed the angels make ready to attack him should he fall from grace. Because of his answer, Abraham, Isaac and Jacob or the archetypes of the soul came to help him as he clung to the Throne of Heaven, that is, his high spiritual state. God appeared to relent and listen to Moses's further argument that the inhabitants of the Earth would say, if the Israelites were destroyed, that the whole operation had no spiritual significance. All mankind would then believe that it was not intended for anyone to be brought out of bondage of the lower Worlds and no one, not even the wise and hopeful, would seek the Garden of Eden and Heaven ever again. At this point the Divine appears to turn the Face of Severity away and, indeed, the text Exodus 32:14 speaks of YAHVEH (the Merciful aspect) repenting of the evil intended towards His people. This term, 'Thy' people, used to Moses, is reversed as the Israelites, for better or worse, are accepted once more by God to be the living example of Divine Law in action to all mankind. Having obtained clemency for the Israelites, Moses 'turned and went down from the Mount', with the Tablets of Testimony in his hand. Note the word 'turned'. Anyone who has had any inner experience will recognise this moment of rotation before coming back into the lower Worlds.

On his way down Moses met Joshua, who had been waiting all the time just below, and together they descended out of the realm of the Spirit and into the psychological World where they stood above and some distance from the physical realm of the camp. Joshua, who did not know what Moses knew, interpreted the hubbub below as warlike cries but Moses disabused him as they approached ground level. Joshua, waiting obediently between the upper and lower Worlds, had been granted a special status during the time on the Mountain but this had placed him out of touch with events above and below. Legend says that, at this point, Moses turned back when he perceived the physical reality of what had happened but the seventy Elders pursued him to take possession of the wondrous tablets. As he miraculously flew before them he saw the Divine Words vanish from the Tablets and they became so unbearably heavy that they fell to earth and were shattered.

When a deeply angered and dismayed Moses walked into the camp and saw the people in revelry about the Golden Calf, he knew that God had given him the task of applying judgement. Nothing less would do but to cut out all the corrupted elements in the community so that the people as a whole might have another chance of redemption. For the individual, this means that not only does he take on the responsibility for his actions and deals with them but that no situation is without hope, however disastrous. God is indeed merciful.

39. Justice and Mercy
EXODUS 32

According to the rabbinical view, the episode of the Golden Calf was equal to the sin of Adam and its consequence was as great for the Israelites down the generations. Much discussion of the incident has taken place over the centuries and, while the mixed multitudes, the influence of the two Egyptian magicians and the cunning of Satan are blamed, the responsibility was always returned to the Israelites themselves for entertaining indiscipline and corruption. This sense of Judgement explains the strictness associated with Jewish Law. However, the fear of consequence was not always enough to deter and the Israelites repeatedly forgot their defection and its lesson, subsequently to suffer again and again, just as an individual does when he repeatedly ignores spiritual law.

The first act of *Teshuvah* or return that Moses carried out was the burning of the Golden Calf. Now fire is the Divine element and so the form and substance of the Calf was dissolved back into the most primeval state. The ashes were then ground into fine powder and strewn upon water which the Children of Israel were then made to drink. Water is the element of Formation or the psyche and so the Israelites had to digest psychologically what they had created, formed and made so as never to forget their idolatrous action. According to tradition, many who denied worshipping the Golden Calf died on drinking the water; when the cleansing process began to work within them, it was too much for their corrupted systems. Seen in the individual, a dishonest psychological resistance to what might be seen as a form of psychotherapy can choke, with lies, the possibility of repentance and therefore the vitality of the psyche. This can cause the cessation of growth for that life.

After this incident Moses then turned to Aaron and interrogated him closely as to his reasons for allowing the Calf incident to happen. Aaron explained how the people were anxious for some, any, action in their boredom of waiting. The most agitated had come to him demanding that he should make them a god which would go before them because Moses was no longer with them. Aaron then told how he had tried to offset any such action by the ornament device, hoping that Moses would return in time. This had delayed events but he had finally been unable to stop the making of the Calf, even though he tried to generate a sense of shame in them. Such a reproach, however, had the opposite effect. Everything suddenly became perverse. Moses listened to all this and then issued the following edict to the Israelites: 'Who is on the Lord's side, let him come unto me'. At this all the men of his own tribe of Levi gathered round him. These he made judges on his own responsibility.

At the individual level we see here the self-analysis after an orgy of indiscipline and dissipation. Interrogation of the responsible elements of the psyche helps to identify the causes of the trouble. When these have been located they have to be severely dealt with or the balance and health of the psyche as a whole is threatened. This is done by the sefirah of Judgement in the psyche, represented by the appointed Levites who carry out the chastisement of Israel.

In the action described in the scripture, brother kills brother and neighbour his neighbour, that is, those inter-related aspects of the psyche that caused the trouble, such as certain negating attitudes born of destructive thoughts and feelings. The Levites in this operation act as the executioners of Severity under obedience, discipline and loyalty to the overall aim of Moses who is the only factor within the situation to perceive what has to be done, objectively and without hesitation. This is the quality of Tiferet, the Seat of Solomon. Seen historically, the killing of 3,000 people seems brutal and uncompromising but we must remember that this is an account of crisis both within a nation and an individual at a most decisive point in their evolution. Severity in such a dangerous situation is sometimes the only way to alter a course of self-destruction and unblock the flow of progress impeded by habits and reactions resistant to change. When perceived in the long view, the severe application of discipline, another quality of Judgement, is seen to balance an excessive Mercy, or tolerance towards evil and chaos which can result in the loss of everything worked for and even death. Many people, when confronted with a deadly habit like excessive drink, often accept a strict regime of abstinence as the only way to avoid the inevitable result of becoming alcoholic. In spiritual matters, the discipline is deeper and more stringent because the results of a misdemeanour can affect several lives.

Justice and Mercy

Here it might be useful to consider the Biblical understanding of Justice and Mercy. While the Old Testament contains much violence, it must be recalled that its basis is the history of a people who, like the Americans, fought with native populations and amongst themselves. However, because there is the spiritual dimension, the conflicts epitomise the struggle between good and evil within and between individuals and nations; they are indeed sometimes called the Wars of the Lord in spite of, to us, their barbarity. There is, however, in contrast to these episodes of severity, much in the Old Testament and in Talmudic commentary that is concerned with Mercy. Consider Joseph's forgiveness of his brothers and David's relationship with Saul. Moreover, in spite of the injunction of an eye for an eye, few people were executed by the rabbinical judiciary in ancient times without conclusive evidence. The presence of Wisdom, Understanding, Knowledge and Mercy is certainly borne out by most of the material in the Bible. Indeed it would never have been accepted as sacred if it did not contain the element of Love to balance Justice. The twenty-third Psalm illustrates this balance well.

Seen from a Kabbalistic viewpoint, what appears in the short term to be Severe, in the long run invariably turns out to be an act of Mercy as each quality is balanced by the other when perceived in terms of the sefirotic Tree. Thus, while a man may cause suffering to another, they will both receive their reward and punishment, if not immediately then later, perhaps in the next life when their positions may be reversed to give them a chance to resolve their problem. Out of Justice comes Mercy.

The lesson of the Golden Calf was not to be wasted. On the day after the slaughter Moses said, 'You have sinned a great sin and now I will go up unto the Lord. Perhaps I shall make atonement for your sin'. Moses then left a repentant people below to ponder their situation while he ascended once more towards the place of God.

40. Consequences
EXODUS 32-33

'And Moses returned unto YAHVEH'. This simple statement contains great implication. It speaks of the facility open to Moses although it has been withdrawn from the Children of Israel. Such accessibility to the Divine is rare and only occurs through a very special external circumstance or a remarkable inner development. According to the oral tradition, there were only seven just men in Israel at that time who were worthy of approaching the higher Worlds. They were Moses, Aaron and his two sons, Eleazer, Ithamar, Phinehas his grandson, Joshua and Caleb. Of these only Moses was capable of direct contact with the Divine at this point. Seen as an analogue of one person, these righteous men might be perceived as those parts of the psyche that had attained some degree of purity. As a group they are related by family or loyalty. This can be perceived as the coalescing of a stable centre within the turbulent struggles of the camp of the psyche.

Now Moses, having climbed the Holy Mountain with these Elders, left them below while he went up into the place where the three highest Worlds meet. There he said to God, 'This people has sinned a great sin. They have made for themselves a god of gold'. That is, they have (the Hebrew word for sin means) 'missed the mark' and worshipped a material image of Existence. This is the situation for those bound by a sensual view of the Universe. Its result is the lowest kind of appreciation of reality based upon nothing but an egocentric view. For example, a deep devotion to physical possessions or worship of worldly status is, for most people, the extension and projection of ego love or one's personal Golden Calf. For the person interested in developing his Soul, such exclusive preoccupations preclude any possibility of spiritual evolution. The sin is particularly bad for one who, like the Israelites, has been shown the way but chooses, like them, to turn his back upon the Covenant. This is, it must be repeated, to become ignorant in the full sense of ignoring what was placed before one. It is indeed a great sin to sin.

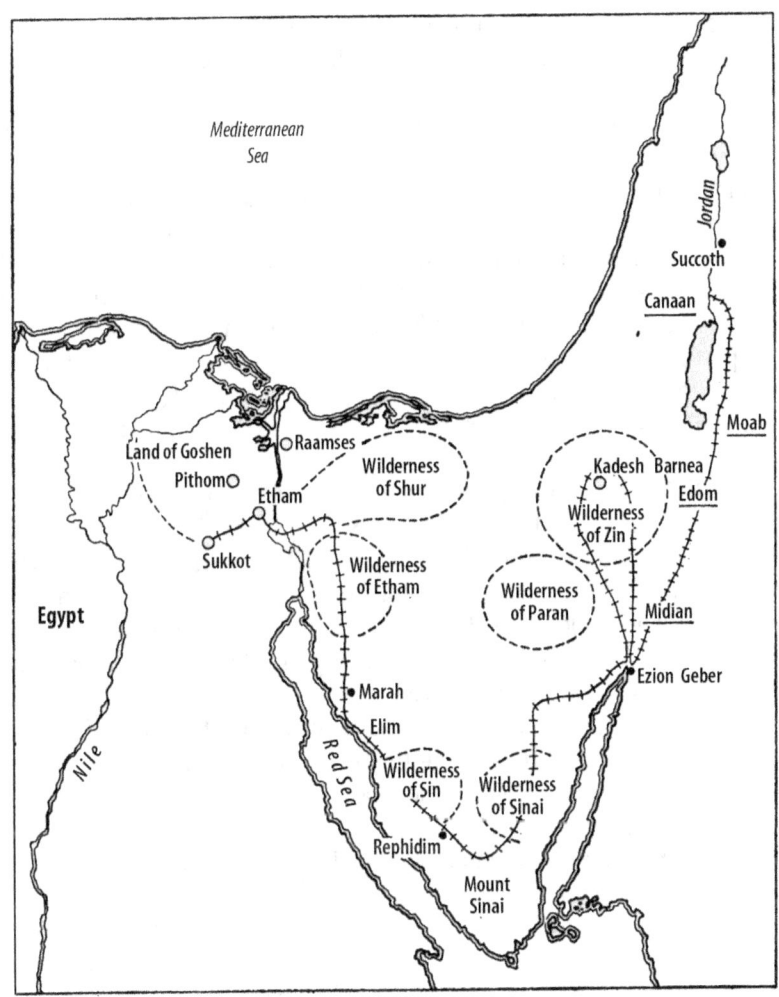

Figure 38 – PLACES
The names of the sites where the Israelites camped are very significant. The name Etham, for example, means Desolation, while Rephidim *can be translated as Rest. These are recognisable stages to those on the Path. The word* Sinai *means a 'Higher Cliff' or 'Superior Level' while Ezion Geber can be interpreted as 'Backbone'. This suggests that the Israelites had developed a strong collective identity meaning that they were, by then, a unified people.*

Moses then said, 'If Thou wilt forgive them, forgive. But if not, blot out my name, I pray, from Thy book which Thou hast written'. Upon this verse there is much interesting oral teaching. According to tradition, before the Throne of Glory are a Book of Life and a Book of Death. Into these are inscribed all the deeds of the creatures in Existence, especially those of the human race which, having free will, can choose good or evil. These two Books are opened for ten days at the beginning of each New Year for the consideration of who will live and who will die during the next twelve months. This process of Judgement and Mercy is continuous throughout Time until the End of Days when the total performance is assessed on the Last Day when every creature in all the Worlds comes before the Lord to present its report on how it fulfilled the mission for which it was created, so that God might behold God.

The Divine reply to Moses's question is, 'Whosoever has sinned against Me, him will I blot out of My Book'. In this is the Teaching on the direct opposition to the Divine Will. This is the sin of a person who knows what he is doing, as against one who is still in a state of innocence. The undeveloped soul acts blindly without experience or knowledge and therefore is not fully responsible. But the individual who sins against God is perceived as being responsible for his own actions because he has reached some level of spiritual maturity. It is therefore much graver Judgement that is applied. Here the most severe sentence, of being taken out of the Book of Life, is to be given for the highest rebellion.

The chapter, however, ends with a blend of Mercy and Justice. Moses is told to lead the people towards the Promised Land. 'But the day will come', the Lord says, 'when I shall visit upon them their sin'. (Note, the word 'visit' is used in the original Hebrew, not 'punish'.) This means the choosing of a moment which will teach the Israelites a lesson about their defection. Anyone who has practised a spiritual discipline has this experience of Karmic law. However, it must be said that it is never applied without Mercy, for the moment the lesson has been learnt, the severity stops. The operation of Justice and Mercy is not to destroy but to correct balance, educate the soul, teach cosmic law and reveal Divine Grace. One rule is that, should an individual recognise his misdemeanour and repent, then the laws of reward and punishment will be adjusted by the Holy One who forgives all who turn towards the Divine.

The next chapter opens with the restatement of God's intention concerning Israel. This is the response to their repentance. Added to the promise of the Land of milk and honey and the sending of an angel before them to drive out their enemies is the fact that the Holy Presence will no longer be with them. This symbolic degradation is set out in Biblical legend which tells how, on the first day of revelation, the Israelites received weapons with the Names of God engraved on them and purple robes. The purple robes or a developed psyche represent a mastery of the World of Formation while the weapons are instruments of control in that World. Later occultists were to imitate these symbols in magical robes and weapons. Because of the Israelites' defection during their initiation, these Grace-given powers were removed by the angels.

Such psychic skills as clairaudience may be acquired by very hard work upon the higher centres of the psyche and are deliberately cultivated by occultists. However, for the spiritual aspirant they are developed naturally as the psyche becomes more refined and sensitised. These faculties include healing, the projection of the consciousness to other places so as to hear or see distant events, interior visions and anticipation of future events. In kabbalistic work these gifts are considered to be the normal way of perceiving the upper and subtler Worlds. They are not to be used for occult or magical manipulation of those below. Indeed, in the Talmud the Rabbis say, 'He who practises magic will not enter Heaven'. This means that a person who devotes himself to operating in the World of Formation will be trapped there by the fascination of magic and will not progress into the World of the Spirit. This is not an uncommon phenomenon in the lower levels of spiritual work. As Biblical folklore tells us that the robes and weapons were removed from the Israelites because they were no longer trustworthy, so it is with individuals who abuse their superior position.

Because of the withdrawal of God's presence, the Israelites went into deep mourning. They collapsed under the Divine words 'you are a stubborn people and I may destroy you at any moment if I AM with you'. Indeed, the depth of their repentance, legend reports, made them take off the ornaments acquired in Egypt and they did not wear them any more in the desert. In this act the ego relinquished what it had been given by the lower Worlds which was used for personal vanity. Here began the process of purification as they waited to hear what the Divine would do with them. When Moses came down from the Mountain he withdrew from the Israelites and pitched a tent outside the camp, symbolising how a separation and removal of direct Grace had occurred. This tent, the Israelites knew, was the only place on Earth where the Divine would reside, for each one, it is recorded, saw from his own doorway the Cloud of the Holy Spirit descend upon the Tent of Meeting, as it came to be called. Here Moses spoke with God 'as a man speaks to his friend'.

EXPERIENCE

41. Illumination
EXODUS 33

The conversation between God and Moses in the Tent of Meeting outside the camp may be considered as a metaphor of the dialogue within an individual between Thou and I. The level at which it takes place would be between the self, where the three lower Worlds meet, and the place where the three upper Worlds meet. This position is the sefirah at the very centre of Jacob's Ladder which acts both as the Knowledge of the psyche and the Foundation of the spirit. This station is also associated with the Archangel Gabriel who is the Annunciator. Here, too, is the place of the Holy Spirit as it manifests to the psyche. The kabbalistic significance of this position is that it enables a man to hear and even see into the upper Worlds, even though he is still in the flesh. Moreover, it facilitates his communication with the Divine at the Crown of his psyche. Thus it was possible for Moses to converse with God while at ground level in the lower Worlds.

The Tent of Meeting became the place also where the Children of Israel came to Moses for advice and intercession on their behalf; here, beyond the frontier of their mundane camp life, was a sacred space where their teacher could enter into contact with the Divine to petition and praise for them. The parallel may be seen in the individual as the ego perceives the developing soul rise up to enter into a spiritual conversation in which it cannot directly participate. Experience shows that such dialogues often go on deep within the unconscious, although the ego can sometimes sense some hint of what is going on by the peace or disturbance precipitated by interior changes. During the time Moses was not in the Tent Joshua, his young assistant, remained on watch as he had on the mountain. He was already being trained to be Moses's successor. The same occurs within the individual as the as-yet inexperienced spiritual aspect of the self is trusted to watch and follow.

'Moses said to the Lord:' (Exodus 33:12) 'Thou didst lead this people up, but Thou has not told me whom Thou wilt send me [to lead us]. Thou has said to me, "I know thee by name and Thou hast found favour in My eyes." If I have found favour let me know Thy ways that I may know Thee.' This double request is most revealing of the process of spiritual instruction. The first is concerned with a guide. If the Lord will not accompany the people, who then will help them? Moses obviously does not see himself as the guide either because, as the Bible later notes, he is a humble man or because, while he is capable of prophetic revelation, he is not yet a man of secure inner knowledge: although he is leader of the people, he can only assume the place of the self but not hold it as a permanent state. This also symbolises the role of any teacher as the makeshift self of the disciple until the Jacob in the disciple, the psychological self, becomes transformed into Israel, the spiritual self.

The second question is concerned with being known by God. To be known by name is to be individually acknowledged and here Moses claims, by this privilege, to be shown the innermost ways that he might come to know God. In answer to the question 'Who will be the guide of the people?' the Lord says, 'My Presence shall go with you in person'. But Moses is unsure of the meaning of this because the Lord has said He will not travel with the people and Moses asks for clarification, saying, 'How will it be known Thou art with us except that Thou go with us?' Here Moses seeks to draw out God's Mercy into the open that the Israelites and the world at large may perceive it. But the Lord, indicating a difference in Divine Ways, avoids a direct answer and speaks only of regard for Moses by repeating that he is known by name. Here is a chain by which all esoteric teaching is imparted. The Divine instructs the teacher or higher psyche which passes on knowledge in an intelligible form to those below in ordinary consciousness.

Biblical legend tells us that Moses's next stage of instruction was to be shown the treasures that are stored up for those who behave with integrity and charity, that is, with Justice and Mercy. He saw also that rewards were destined for those who failed their mission as well as those who completed their task. This puzzled Moses until he was reminded that Divine Ways are not like man's. The Lord is gracious to whom the Divine wishes to be gracious. The Lord, perceiving Moses's perplexity, demonstrated how sometimes the appearance of reward and punishment is misleading to the unperceptive eye as Moses, in clairvoyant vision, had a real-life incident played out before him. A man was killed without apparent reason until it was revealed that this violent death was the result of a previous crime. As a result the dead man's property was then restored to its original owner, from whom it had been stolen. Thus, through a chain of apparently unconnected events, Justice and Mercy brought about equilibrium in the world.

Moses not only saw the laws of reward and punishment at work but was allowed, legend tells us, to glimpse deep into the future where he saw every generation and its spiritual leaders. This showed him how the world was governed, not by the power of physical might or psychological willpower, but by spiritual and cosmic forces that operated according to the Heavenly watchfulness of Providence — unless the Divine chose to intervene. By such an act it was revealed that Divinity would grant Grace even to the undeserving if they prayed for mercy, having acknowledged their stupidity.

At the end of this lesson Moses asked that he be shown the Divine Glory. In Kabbalistic terms, he wished to view the World of Emanation without the veiling of the lower Worlds. The reply was that he would not be allowed to see the Divine Light directly because it would destroy his acquired individuality. Only those who were prepared to sacrifice their sense of self in the presence of Eternity could be considered ready for this stage of union. For 'no man may See the Face of God and live'. Besides, Moses had work to do below on Earth. However, Moses would be granted an oblique vision of the Glory by being placed in a cleft of the Rock. The word *Hatsur* is used in the text. Kabbalistically it indicates the legendary Rock of Shetiyah which is 'the Foundation Stone of the World'. Besides being Jacob's pillow when he saw the Great Ladder of Heaven, it is the Rock which the Creator cast into the Abyss at the beginning of Creation to act as the connection between Divinity and the lower Worlds. Moses was to be placed within this Rock which was, according to legend, to form the base of Solomon's Temple. From its protection he would glimpse the hind part of the Glory of God.

42. *Enlightenment*
EXODUS 34

Before going up the Holy Mountain, Moses was instructed to cut two stone tablets like the first that had been broken. These humanly made Tables would replace the Divinely created ones. Here we see the teaching about Grace and Merit in which the Will of God comes down to meet and fuse with the work of man rising from below. 'Be ready by morning', Moses is told, 'and come up in the morning'. This, in kabbalistic terms, is that portion of the day predominated by Mercy, energy and love, as against the evening which is the time of Justice, reflection and form. 'Then in the morning go up Mount Sinai; and present thyself to Me upon the top of the Mountain'. There then follows the instruction that no other creature must be on the Mountain.

The ascent of the Holy Mountain is, in Kabbalah, carried out in two main phases. The first is the seven stages of what are called the lower Halls. These are the psychological levels that correspond to the angelic World of Formation. It consists of moving out of the body, through the ego, beyond thoughts, feelings and action into an awakening state before passing into the soul level which leads on to the level of the spirit and contact with the Divine. The second stage begins at the transit point of the self where the soul takes the aspirant up through the seven greater Halls of Spiritual Devotion, Purity, Sincerity, Godliness, Holiness, Sacredness and so into the Presence where, according to tradition, Moses entered the cleft in the rock at the mountain's top. (This is the same cave where Elijah was to be when the Divine Glory was revealed to him.) As he ascended up through the Worlds, Moses was again shown all the celestial hierarchies of angels and archangels. 'How is it', they protested, 'that we who serve the Divine day and night may not be permitted to see the Glory of Azilut?' Because of this hostility, Moses had to be protected from the celestials who resented any creature of the earth superseding them in favour. This tells us that any journey up through the Worlds involves great dangers as tests are applied to the person as he encounters psychological and cosmic archetypes. Several books upon dealing with these levels and their angelic guardians are to be found in kabbalistic literature. Often repeated is the rule that no human may pass through these heavenly creatures until he is more than equal to them. This applies inwardly and outwardly and preserves any unwary intruder into these Worlds from being shattered by massive psychological and spiritual forces. It moreover safeguards against any abuse by those who try to play with these psychic or cosmic energies. Occasionally, psychologically burnt and spiritually blasted individuals are met with; Aaron's two sons dying in the sanctuary illustrate the point. When the time came for Moses to see the Glory, God is reported to have said, 'When I revealed Myself to thee in the Burning Bush thou didst not wish to look upon Me; now thou art willing, and I AM not'. In this is the statement that for every individual there is one instant in life when the Glory may be seen without the danger. These acts of Grace, often coming at critical points in life, leave the person utterly changed in his attitude towards Existence.

As the Cloud of Creation descended over the Rock, the Bible records, '*Vayityatsav imo sham*'. 'And He stood there with him, and proclaimed the Name'. And YAHVEH passed before his face. Legend says that at this point the Rock closed in upon Moses and he perceived only the reflection of the passing Glory as the following was proclaimed:

YAHVEH YAHVEH
GOD
MERCIFUL AND GRACIOUS
LONG SUFFERING
GREAT IN KINDNESS
AND TRUTH
KEEPING KINDNESS FOR THOUSANDS
FORGIVING INIQUITY AND TRANSGRESSION
AND SIN
BUT WHO WILL BY NO MEANS CLEAR
THE GUILT, VISITING THE INIQUITY OF
THE FATHER UPON THE CHILDREN
UNTO THE THIRD AND FOURTH *[generation?]*

The foregoing verses are known in Kabbalah as the thirteen Attributes or Qualities of Mercy. According to some they represent the three unseen *Zahzahot* or Hidden Splendours and the Ten Sefirot. Others see them as the manifestation of the upper Divine Face of Mercy called the LONG SUFFERING and the lower or Short Face of Severity symbolised by the last verse. Perceived as the most majestic statement after the Decalogue of the Commandments, the thirteen Qualities have been preserved in the Jewish liturgy to be recited on solemn holidays, especially those associated with penitence such as the Day of Atonement. According to the Talmud, the recitation of them before the Lord will precipitate forgiveness and no one who has made the Covenant will be turned away empty-handed. However, the implication is that the petitioner has reached a degree of development or ascent where he is indeed before the Throne of Glory, as Moses was where he stood. (Again, in the original Hebrew there is no word about generation.)

Moses, at this moment of enlightenment, legend relates, bowed his head towards the earth as he remembered that his substance, like that of Adam, was of clay, and said, 'If now I have found Grace in Thy sight, O ADONAI, Let My LORD, I pray Thee, go among us, for we are a stiff-necked people. Pardon our iniquities, our sin, and take us as Thine inheritance'.

The Divine response to Moses's request was to renew the Covenant with Israel before all the people. In this would be the hope and redemption for all; Mankind will perceive that, in spite of Israel's failure, the Lord would forgive although each generation must face its lessons under the laws of cosmic Justice. Thus, with the severity that is to follow the Israelites in the desert comes a strengthening and preservation of purity and integrity as corruption and laxity die and perversion, rebellion and deception perish. Divine Justice and Rigour are not so much the Qualities of Fear and Retribution but a strictness that is sometimes required to bring an individual or people back from a course of total disaster.

'I will do wonders', said the Lord, 'such as have not been done in all the Earth; not in any nation. And all the surrounding people shall see the work of the Lord. For it is an awesome thing that I shall do for you'. In this promise the Divine re-establishes the connection after having withdrawn it from the Israelites. In an individual life this experience of Mercy is paralleled. Often, despite foolish error or deliberate resistance, many have found that once they have admitted their deviation, Divine Grace has again flowed to heal suffering and make good the damage done by ego or even the self when it is set against the Way of Heaven.

43. Radiance
EXODUS 34

After the revelation of the Thirteen Qualities of Mercy, the scripture changes tempo as it repeats the Divine promise to aid the Israelites to take the land into which they will come, warning them to make no covenant with the inhabitants lest they be corrupted by them.

Indeed, the Israelites are told to destroy all the religious institutions they find. The text then becomes a blend of the Ten Commandments and extracts from the Priestly Code, suggesting that this passage was inserted later by scribes who did not understand the nature of the upper Worlds. Indeed, they seem, again, concerned with enhancing priestly authority by placing their preoccupation with festival and sacrifice immediately after Moses's profound experience. There has been much scholarly discussion over the centuries about, say, the verse on not boiling a kid in its mother's milk but a little common sense, plus some deep experience, indicates that most of the wordy analyses are merely learned solutions when it is obviously a symbol for spiritual corruption—which is ironic in this context. Learning, without esoteric knowledge, cannot tell the difference between theory and reality. Only direct personal experience can separate opinion from truth, that is, inner knowledge.

Moses, both the Bible and folklore tell us, stayed for forty days and nights on the Mountain. During this time he was taught all the Torah, that is those things that are to be revealed and those things not to be revealed. The reason why it is said all the teaching was given is because the term 'forty days and nights' is used. In Kabbalah this phrase means that Moses experienced all forty sefirot of the four Worlds in both their imparting and receptive aspects. During this time he neither ate nor drank because he was sustained by the same substance that feeds the angelic beings. This, Tradition says, is the Emanation of the Shekhinah, the Light proceeding from the World of Emanation. Thus it was that Moses slowly acquired the radiance that was to shine out from his face when he descended the Mountain.

Seen in individual terms, when a person reaches Moses's level of Enlightenment he has risen out of the mundane state of the body through the psychological World to the place where the three upper Worlds meet. Here the Divine Glory radiates down upon his spirit and percolates his psychological organism. The greater the depth and duration of exposure to the upper Worlds, the deeper and longer the radiance remains. In the case of those in sustained contact, like the Buddha, the radiance becomes a permanent feature. In lesser beings such as saints and sages the phenomenon is not so marked, although it is recorded as a halo or an aura that is sensed, if not seen, by ordinary mortals. Here we have the process by which the Divine World penetrates the lower three vehicles of one who is purified enough to allow Emanation to shine through his being. The scripture goes on to describe the phenomenon.

'And it came to pass when Moses came down from Mount Sinai with the two Tables of Testimony in his hand that he did not know that the skin of his face shone because he had been speaking with the Lord' (Exodus 34:29). Legend describes how Aaron and the people were afraid of Moses because, before they had sinned, they were able to gaze at the seven fiery sheaths of the Glory but now they could not even look upon a man who had been in its Presence because of the profound awe they felt on seeing the light radiate from Moses's countenance. Perceived in individual experience, this phenomenon may be witnessed after a deep meditation session under esoteric discipline when certain people radiate a glow that is perceptible to everybody else. The quality of the radiance is extraordinary purity and gentle power that reveals the soul of the person. The light usually fades as the psyche and then bodily activities overlay the light and enclose it in mood and materiality. A similar phenomenon occurs with the new-born. They lose a lucidity of being as their dense bodies and fumbling psyches cloud the spirit and overshadow the innermost radiance as they come down to earth to be fully incarnated.

Moses, having reached the physical World, put a veil over his face. This is a metaphor for screening the interior radiance by the mask of the ego. The reason for this is that in life the ego not only acts as the shutter between the outside world and the inner, to prevent the coarser levels entering into the psyche, but also protects the inner from blinding the outer, as any mutual eye contact may do. When one is in the presence of a great being, the discrepancies of one's own nature are illuminated by contrast and this can be extremely painful. Both Jesus

Figure 39—ENLIGHTENMENT
When Moses came down from Mount Sinai, his face shone with such inner brilliance that he had to cover it, for it blinded people. This phenomenon is not uncommon with great spiritual masters. Because of this, they hide their light behind the mask of personality. This is sometimes necessary because such charisma enrages the shadow side of some who seek to obliterate the Truth. Various great sages and saints have found this to their cost. (Rev.T. Bankes's Bible, 19th century).

and Socrates were penalised by those they often inadvertently exposed as frauds by their clarity of vision. A teacher, therefore, will often shield his students from his full light out of consideration until they can bear to see themselves. Meanwhile, instruction comes from behind a veil. Pythagoras and Mahomet are reported to have taught this way.

Tradition says that Moses taught according to a definite method whose rationale should be recognisable by now. First he instructed Aaron and then his two sons, while Aaron listened a second time. After this he taught the Elders concerning the teaching about God, the World and Man with Aaron and his two sons looking on. Then he taught the people with all those who had been instructed listening in. Thus Aaron had heard it four times, one for each level of reality. Then Moses withdrew and Aaron repeated what he had learned, as did his sons, the Elders and the people until everyone had heard it four times. In this way they were shown the Teaching in the terms of each of the Worlds and at the four levels of physical, psychological, spiritual and Divine operation. How much was comprehended is to be assessed by one's own performance when being instructed. Without doubt the different parts of one's make-up receive knowledge in different ways, so that the Teaching may have a practical application, a psychological appeal, resonate spiritually and even give one a moment of Divine experience. Each level will respond in its own way, absorbing much unconsciously, until it is recalled when needed by the individual at a particularly relevant point.

While Moses wore the veil below before the people, he removed it when he went up before the Lord. This describes symbolically how the veil was transformed from a protector into an impediment when Moses himself became the student. By discarding the veil, which is related to the Knowledge of the psyche and the Foundation of the Spirit, he could open up to receive instruction from the Highest. In this condition he was in a state of *Kibal* or receiving; which is the root word of Kabbalah. After he had been taught, Moses turned from receiving from above to imparting to below. First, however, he covered his face so as not to discourage the people from the Work of Unification, as it came to be called. This was not only the joining of the different tribes into a Nation but also the work that brings all parts of an individual together and unites all the Worlds.

WORK

44. Organisation and Direction
EXODUS 35

Revelation always precedes tradition, it cannot be the other way round. Out of Revelation comes the oral line which then becomes the written and ritual tradition. In this way the transmission of the Teaching follows the doctrine of the Four Worlds in its descent from Divine Will, through spiritual knowledge and psychological form into physical manifestation. Thus it was when Moses began to transmit the instructions concerning the Tabernacle which were already in existence in the upper Worlds.

In the beginning of Exodus chapter 35 Moses calls all the community together and addresses them. This can be seen in the individual as the self bringing the psyche and body into consciousness so as to consider the aim of making the Tabernacle. Moses began by stating the strict rules of the exercise and how it must follow the laws of Creation with its periodic rest for recreation and reflection. Then, softening, he indicated that whosoever wished with a willing heart could make some contribution both in labour and material. This meant that not only was the middle pillar of Consciousness involved but the right pillar of Energy and the left pillar of Matter. In this way the Lightning Flash of the Crown zigzagged down from will, through the intellect and emotion into the kingdom of the body as it stood in the World of Action and Elements. Grace, Mercy and Justice were to be earthed.

The materials have already been described in detail but the way in which the whole lay-out of what is needed is repeated indicates an ordering in a lower world as the design specification begins to come into manifestation. The people, having been given the physical requirements for building the Tabernacle, then went back to their camps, collected what materials they had and gave them as a free-will offering. This was absolutely vital, otherwise the Work would have no significance to them or the Tabernacle. Indeed any effort carried out under coercion, be it by external pressure on the ego, internal pride of the self, under the threat of fear or fascination of love, is invalid. The moment free will goes, the Work ceases to be worship and becomes labour, then routine drudgery. Under these conditions, nothing is given, but only taken.

The text says that every man and woman brought a personal ornament. These individual sacrifices represent the contribution of the body. The psyche gave its gifts when the men and women offered their special skills, the former practising the masculine arts, the latter the feminine. In this way the talents performed a ritual of making, forming and creating sacred objects as materials were hammered, woven, cut, sewn, joined and linked into the various components of the Tabernacle, its furniture and the priestly garments. Here is an analogue of a labour of love that goes on for many years in the Kabbalist as he works at the Tabernacle of himself to create, form and make a Holy place within his psyche and body for the soul, spirit and Divinity to reside.

The chiefs of the tribes gave the precious stones for the Ephod and Breast-plate. They also contributed the perfumes and oil for the lamp. This tells us how the animal part of the people or individual gave of treasures that had been accumulated in life. These might be seen in the princely talents, such as the ability to organise, the gift to inspire confidence or the possession of great determination.

At this point Moses announced to the Israelites that Bezalel had been especially chosen to implement the Work because he who was in the shadow of God was filled with the Spirit of ELOHIM, 'in Wisdom and in Understanding and Knowledge'. Bezalel would co-ordinate; as the Hebrew text puts it, '*Kol Ish ve Isba*' 'Every man and woman', '*Asheh nadav libam otam*' 'Whose heart made them willing'. Here are the pillars at work in harmony.

The master craftsman Bezalel and his assistants then began to supervise the construction of the Tabernacle, instructing by Divine inspiration the way the design was to be executed. According to tradition, Bezalel knew the form of the design in greater detail than Moses. This was because he received his inspiration at the lower levels of Existence where the laws are more complex and therefore more detailed in their manifestation; that is, the working-out of the heavenly scheme at ground level paid more attention to particulars because, in the lowest World, the point of manifestation operates through a specific time and place. The intuitive but practical view of Bezalel from below is symbolised by a legendary conversation with Moses, who asked him in what order he should build the Tabernacle. Unlike the Divine plan that began with the Ark, Bezalel proposed to build the Tabernacle first, that is from the outer and lower levels in towards the centre and highest. Here is an individual working from his exterior consciousness into his interior, from the particular to the general. This is the way of man as against the Divine.

45. Construction Work
EXODUS 36

The actual construction of the Tabernacle and its contents is described in great detail over several chapters in Exodus. It is almost a repetition of the specification passages but not quite. It begins with the collecting of the materials and then the assembling of all the craftsmen to come under the direction of Bezalel and his assistant Aholiab, who would see 'that the work shall be carried out exactly as the Lord commanded'. Once more contributions had been gathered than were actually needed, the Work was begun on the Tabernacle's ten hangings of blue, purple and red yarn woven into white linen. A symbol of the Ten Sefirot is usually the first thing with which the student Kabbalist has to make himself familiar. Often he has to construct a diagram for himself so as actually to materialise and experience the Model upon which the four Worlds of Existence are based. Having woven the ten hangings, the Israelites then went on to join them together, by loops and fastenings, until they became, as the Hebrew text says, *ehad*, one, or whole. This is the first stage of the sefirot coming into manifestation as they did at the beginning of Existence.

After the protective coverings of goats' hair, rams' hides and porpoise skins had been made to represent the three lower Worlds, the wooden part of the Tabernacle was constructed. This was carried out according to a definite sequence which reminds anyone who has been under a spiritual discipline of the ordered way one is taught the theory and practice of a Tradition piece by piece, as one constructs a Tabernacle within oneself. Take, for example, the bars of the main structure. First five on one side are made and then the five bars on the complementary side are finished, after which the five bars for the end of the Tabernacle are cut. These are then arranged so as to join the wall planks together after they had all been plated with gold. Anyone who observes a construction site must realise that there is a 'critical flow pattern' that governs the work. This pattern is designed to bring in the various elements being assembled at just the right moment, so that they do not get in each other's way or stop the growth of the building. For instance, the installation of a bathroom before the drainage system had been put in would be considered bad design and management; and so it is in spiritual development. There is no short cut without impeding growth or setting the flow pattern of the Soul back until each physical or psychological function has been correctly connected or developed. Thus the flow pattern of the Tabernacle demonstrates in its construction a most important spiritual lesson that things can only be completed when everything else is ready to move on. Many aspirants do not perceive this law and become impatient and even lose faith when Providence seems to be holding back. Nothing occurs outside its time as it is part of a sequence in the great cosmic cycle that unfolds the Grand Design of Existence.

The last elements to be made for the central structure were the Veil, the four inner posts, the screen and its five outer posts. These are composed, like the rest of the Tabernacle, of shittim wood plated with gold, joined by gold hooks, silver and brass sockets and fine linen embroidered with blue, purple and scarlet yarn. This sequence completes and seals in the double and single chambers of the Tabernacle which represent the upper and inner Worlds. The significance of all this for the Israelites is enormous, if the work is carried out as an act of worship. In this way the operation takes on the dimension of transformation as the raw materials being used are lifted out of their crude state into greater refinement. The practice of actually building a sacred structure is a method of teaching used by many Traditions as a way of demonstrating how the lower World can be made to be the receptacle of the higher, as many sacred places with their other-world atmospheres show. This can only be achieved by builders under spiritual direction. The technique is called 'the approach of action' and it is taught either by the example of a teacher or his watching a student perform the motions of an operation with fully conscious attention. This transforms every action into a sacred ritual. No doubt this approach was applied by Bezalel to the Israelite labour force.

If we consider the actual building of the Tabernacle as a metaphor of Work on the body, psyche and spirit it becomes apparent that a new phase is under way in the journey to the Promised Land. Up to now the Israelites have been nurtured. They have been aided from above to escape from bondage, helped cross the Sea of no return and been sustained by Providence in spite of seven minor and one major revolts. Now they are taking on the Work for themselves. While it is true that they follow a design laid out by Heaven, they nevertheless have the choice about the Work. Judging by the care and attention lavished upon the emerging structure, it is clear that they have made the decision to join in the down-flowing creative and up-flowing evolutionary processes to make in the Tabernacle a mirror of the Universe. In its reflection they will see themselves, not only in their individual performance but also in the slowly unifying consciousness that emerges out of such Work. Here is the beginning of the uniting of the Tribes within the community of the psyche as the various elements and facets labour under a greater purpose, even though as yet there are only the scattered components of the Tabernacle being worked on all over the camp.

46. Architect
EXODUS 37-38

Legend tells us that Bezalel had not only the Wisdom of the Torah but also insight into the *Halakah* or sacred regulations when the Teaching was applied to ordinary life. This was possible because, being at the place of the psychological self, he had access to the Worlds above and the Worlds below. This position is also called the station of Devotion and corresponds to the first hall of the *Vilon* or Veil that is drawn back as the self opens up to the realms of Heaven. Such an individual was at the junction point between Creation, the domain of man, and the physical world of energy and matter. Thus could Bezalel connect Heaven and Earth in practical action.

'*Vayaas Bezalel et haAron*'. 'And Bezalel made the Ark'. That is, he manufactured in physical reality the creative idea and formative design that God had willed and called forth. Thus the Ark became fully realised in all the Worlds, seen in individual experience. The making of the Ark requires the greatest attention because it is the place over which the Holy One will hover and to where a person will go deepest in the recesses of his own being. It lies beyond the outer screen of the Soul and the veil of the Spirit. It is, to the individual, the Holy of Holies. Therefore Bezalel, the shadow of God, took it upon himself to make this most sacred of objects while the rest of the Israelites worked upon the Tabernacle.

The Ark was made exactly to the specifications given to Moses. Constructed of shittim wood and covered within and without in pure gold it was executed by his finest workmanship, so that near-perfection was achieved even though the Ark would never be seen by most Israelites once it was in the Holy of Holies. The making of the Mercy Seat, with its Cherubim and their screening wings, from the purest gold refined from what had been brought up out of Egypt, was a symbolic ritual of Transformation. The thousand and one techniques of craft to transform the metal ornaments and vanities out of their old shapes and into new unified form to hold the highest meaning must have taught much to those who aided Bezalel. This was one of many lessons about the dissolution of the Israelites' old conditioning. The gruelling life in the desert had already revealed many useless aspects of their past life but there were many more to be erased, beaten and blasted off for the Israelites had not yet reached the state where anything new could emerge.

The making of the Table and the Candle-stick for the outer sanctuary followed the construction of the Ark. These two objects were also exercises in experiencing deep symbols as they were brought into physical manifestation. The standard of work on these sacred pieces had to be of a refinement only a degree less than that of the Ark. Indeed, the craftsmen employed were most likely graded according to their level of competence and spiritual comprehension—a concept not unfamiliar to the latter-day Temple builders, the Masons. Seen within the individual, this process occurs according to innate laws as different parts of the psyche and body are arranged to perform a hierarchy of tasks. Thus, as every faculty has its place, so each craftsman has his skill and contributes his worth. No-one, seen in the context of the whole, is more valuable than anyone else although each individual has his special station in the organisation.

Under Bezalel's inspiration, the work force produced the highest order of quality as they translated each idea through every stage of beaten, moulded and sewn form to the finished object. Thus the seven branched Candle-stick, the Showbread Table, tongs and fire pans, the Altar of incense and the perfumes to be burned in it were all brought slowly into being by the agency of the human mind, heart and hand.

By the time the Work had got as far as making the great bronze Laver, the moment for constructing the outer Court had come. This is, kabbalistically, precisely the correct point in the critical flow sequence for it corresponds exactly with the interleaving point between lower Formation and upper Action. The Laver represents the ego of the psyche as well as the place of Knowledge of the body, so whoever wrote about the Laver knew of this interpenetration between the lower psyche and the upper body at that place. The Court and its four sides, its panels of linen, sockets, posts and embroidered gates facing east were constructed last in the main sequence of the building.

As the prefabrication stage finished on the Tabernacle, it began to act as the focus on the mass mind of the people, even though it was still to be erected. Suddenly, the people could no longer regard themselves as separate tribes. During this building project they had forgotten their family differences for they had been joined in making something larger than tribal interests. Everyone had given something of their own, either a gift or skill or both. Moreover, they had worked in groups according to craft rather than blood relationship. This had created and formed a new type of unity over and above the vegetable and animal level of their lives. Something new was happening.

Seen in terms of the individual, the process described above occurs within the psyche when sacred Work is done with others in a common high aim under the direction of a spiritual teacher. These special conditions generate a situation with an horizon far above ordinary circumstance and create an atmosphere that brings a sense of union both with the others and within oneself. This phenomenon is common to, and the mark of, any group working on the soul. Under the increasing presence of the Holy Spirit, the inner process of integration sets aside egotistic motivation and encourages the self which begins to serve the Soul which, in turn, aids the cosmic Work of Heaven that seeks to reach down and touch the Earth.

It is at this point that the scripture gives credit and compliment to Bezalel's assistant Aholiab whose name means, it will be recalled, 'Tent of his Father'. He is the physical aspect of the self at the Crown of the Lowest World. The text indicates his practical contribution by saying that he was an engraver and a skilful workman and an embroiderer in the blue, purple and scarlet yarn and in fine linen. Aholiab knew how to work in all the Worlds under the Pavilion of God.

47. Material and Skill
EXODUS 38-39

As if to bring us rapidly down to earth, the latter part of the thirty-eighth chapter of Exodus is concerned with a full list of materials used in the building of the Tabernacle. In it are set out the quantities of gold and silver contributed by the community and by each man over twenty years old. This is recognition of an individual's obligation towards the community which imparts to him the benefits received from the upper Worlds. Also mentioned are the metals of the mineral realm, the linen of the vegetable kingdom and yarn from the animal kingdom which have been raised from their natural condition to be used in the Holy unification of the Worlds. This concept underlies the text as it repeats the types of materials and how they were transformed into the many components of the Tabernacle. The accounting into talents and shekels sets out the cost in weight, so that all may perceive the total treasure given. The Israelites had not realised, until this point, that so much wealth was in their midst. When everything had been collected from every corner of the camp into one place, there had been a transformation. Suddenly a myriad personal baubles had become the great treasure of the people. The lesson of uniting the parts into a whole is demonstrated at the material level in this chapter.

The significance of the above for the individual is not only the issue of how much a person may be prepared to give of his physical possessions, labour, skill and time but also to recognise the shift of scale in the Work and its fruit when the value of such things are given to something greater. Initially there is much resistance as the vegetable level seeks to preserve its personal comforts and the animal its symbols of status. Eventually, unless the Work is left, the Soul takes the possessions of the lower nature and helps to offer them up as sacrifice which, it must be repeated, means to make something sacred. With this comes the resolution of many interior conflicts between the interests of various parts of the body and psyche. The aim is to bring these all together to create a communal fortune that is greater than just the sum of all the contributions.

After the evaluation of the materials, the text goes on to describe the making of the priestly vestments. First the Ephod is made, the three yarns of blue, purple and scarlet being woven into the base of linen. Then the gold is beaten into thin plates that are cut into strips and twisted into braid which is woven into the yarn and linen. This process is long and exacting and requires sustained attention on the part of the seamster who must never forget what he is making or why. This work is quite unlike any professional commission. It is sacred and must be performed in such a way that no profane thoughts, emotions or actions intrude and so contaminate the Work because what occurs in the artisan during the creation, forming and making of an object permeates it for the rest of its existence. The beauty imbued by such conscious work can never be lost as many grace-filled fragments of ancient workmanship still show. Nor can any flaw that has occurred during the creative process be eliminated. Indeed, many great craftsmen have recognised this law and prefer to destroy an object and start again because such a deeply ingrained malformation cannot be rectified. So it is with any Work carried out to reflect the perfection of the Divine World.

The Ephod of the High Priest represents this level within a human being, so it has to be the most perfect workmanship. The making of the rosettes with their engraved cornelian stones was an art demanding the highest kind of conscious Work, for the names of the sons of Israel had to be cut and set out in an esoteric pattern that embodied a metaphysical scheme, an allegorical meaning and a ritualistic function. These three aspects combined the mind, heart and body of the engraver. He had to know the significance of each name and their correspondence in himself as he made the seals or there would be no resonance imparted into the object which, under his eye and hand, would not only crystallise according to the form he gave it but also absorb the physical, psychological and spiritual state he was in. Such artisans could not be ordinary men motivated by money or even pride of craft. It had to be of an order close to Bezalel the Artist of God.

The construction of the Breast-plate develops the theme of the twelve brothers in precious stones that accord to their natures. The carbuncle of Levi, for example, flashes like the lightning of the revelation of wisdom he received. Issachar's sapphire illustrates how he was devoted to the study of the Tablets of the Law which were made of this stone. Joseph's onyx represented the grace and favour of this generous brother. In contrast Gad's stone was crystal which gave the tribe hardness and clarity in battle for right and justice. Legend traces these attributes and those of the other brothers back to Jacob's blessing at the end of Genesis. The jewels, like the names, were then fixed into the Breast-plate according to a definite pattern that defined the laws of relationship between men who reflected the twelve spiritual types of human being.

The manufacture of the gold ropes, rosettes and rings and their fixing to the Ephod are described in great minuteness, so that the construction of the garment is seen to follow a carefully worked-out sequence. The under-garment of blue and the chequered vestment are dealt with very briefly which indicates a reduction of importance for these coats and those made for Aaron's sons. This process is echoed in the individual as he works down from the highest and deepest levels of his being towards the lower parts of himself. However, everything he does is matched against the standard of his greatest moments of realisation which produce the Divine gold from which he weaves his own Ephod each day he works on spirit, soul and body.

The making of a pure gold plate to be set on the turban of Aaron is the final stage of the whole operation. Upon this plate were engraved the words, '*KADOSHLA YAHVEH*', 'HOLY TO YAHVEH'. The plate was then fixed with blue braid, the colour of the World of Creation, to the top of the turban. The meaning of this for the Kabbalist is that the Crown of the Tree of the High Priest is blessed by the *SHEM HA MEFORASH*, the special NAME of God. This title corresponds to the level of the CREATOR at the centre of the Tree of the Divine World. Thus the High Priest within each person can contact, via the Crown of the spirit at the place of the inner Ark, the Holy One Blessed Be He. This is possible because it is said (Exodus 20:24) that where this particular GOD NAME is caused by the Divine to be remembered, there the PRESENCE would come, as promised, into the consciousness of man.

48. Assembly and Consecration
EXODUS 39-40

On the completion of the Work the Israelites brought all the components of the Tabernacle to be assembled. Moses then inspected every part to see that it had been made according to what the Lord had commanded. And so the scripture says, 'They had made'.

Anyone who has constructed something must know what it is like the moment before all the separate elements are joined together. It is the final pause in which to appreciate all that has gone into the making of the object. It is the last time many things will be seen before they will be hidden within the assembly and disappear for ever into the depths of the totality that covers everything in a new dimension of unity. Such a stage occurs in kabbalistic work. For many months, or even years, the theory has been learnt and the practices diligently carried out. One by one, ideas have been understood and exercises mastered. But still they are no more than a repertoire of concepts and techniques. Suddenly there is the edge of a breakthrough. One begins to glimpse what the teacher says and does as all the experience starts to fuse into a set of simple rules. The hours spent studying and performing vanish into a series of moments that bring everything together. One is at the frontier of unity.

Tradition says that Moses did not set the Tabernacle up straight away but delayed for three months, despite the fact that the people wanted to dedicate it at once. In this is repeated a lesson of patience concerning matters of the spirit. For instead of accepting their Teacher's word, which conveyed the Will of God, the Israelites sought to impose their own will over what they had made, despite Moses's instruction that they were to wait until the first of the Hebrew month of Nison. This day, which began the season of Spring, the annual rebirth of Nature, was also the time of the Passover celebration of the Exodus out of Egypt. The people did not recognise the connection between the times and Moses was subjected to much grumbling. This indicated that the people were still not ready for, while the Work had been carried out

Figure 40—PRIESTHOOD
The three garments of the High Priest represent the three upper Worlds within a human being with his body being the Earthly fourth. All of the ritual and objects had a meaning that was intended to represent a sacred principle. The Ark, for example, held the tablets of the Teaching. It was also the place where the Divine Presence hovered during the ceremonies. These were carried out according to a special order so as to raise the consciousness of those who participated in the rituals. (Rev.T. Bankes's Bible, 19th century).

well, some had just been pleased to be occupied or even be entertained. Moreover, while most operated satisfactorily under discipline, the moment there was nothing to do it was clear that these bored Israelites could stir up the others into restlessness and resentment towards their instructor.

This phenomenon is not unknown among those who cannot wait—which is a vital part of esoteric training. Unfortunately, it has to be demonstrated over and over again that the timing of a spiritual event is contingent upon a cosmic schedule and not the will of the individual. This is often ignored by the wilful and will-less aspects of the people, or psyche. The remarks of certain Israelites about Moses spending all their money to serve his own ends while they, the people, were without the benefits of their work is paralleled in the individual and even in a study group in which dissident members at the same stage of breakthrough seek to goad the instructor into some kind of action. Such events reveal many hitherto-unseen motivations and show that there is still a long way to go in a personal discipline. It is often at this point that people break away from the Work because there is nothing in it for them. Frequently they slander their instructor and seek to split the unity of the group because they think they know better than the experienced leader.

Legend tells how such people went to Bezalel and asked him to set up the Tabernacle, so that the Shekhinah might descend upon them and they dwell with the angels. But even he who had built the complex could not raise it beyond the stage of being a collection of components ready for assembly. This illustrates how even the psychological self, however skilled in the arts of the lower Worlds of form and material, cannot command the spiritual World above to unify the whole. At this failure, we are told, some Israelites became very angry and spoke openly against Moses, saying they had spent much time and money as well as work on the Tabernacle and what had they got to show for it?

This phenomenon also occurs among those who expect results from spiritual labour. They do not work as service but perform to obtain special privileges. They consider their work to be like that done in the lower Worlds where a person earns a physical reward or acquires a psychological skill. In Kabbalah, the Work at this level is done for its own sake. It is undertaken because it is recognised that Providence already has given an abundance of physical, psychological and spiritual gifts. With this in mind, the Kabbalist pays his debts to the Universe by being ready to aid in the Work of Unification.

The legend goes on to say that all the people then went to Moses and asked him why the Tabernacle could not be set up, not even by Bezalel. Had they done something wrong, been shoddy in their work or omitted something? Moses replied that there was nothing wrong with the Tabernacle or anything that was to go into it. However, he grieved secretly because even he could not understand at this point why the setting-up had been so long delayed. This shows that, while Moses had his moments of contact with the Divine, when he was not in communion he too sank down through the Worlds to his optimum level of being the prophetic complement to Aaron at the Nezah position of Yezirah. This meant that even he did not always remember what he had been told or comprehend its meaning when he descended to the Yesodic position of ego. Fortunately he still retained his faith and so was constant, even in his perplexity. Such a state of wakefulness and then forgetfulness sometimes occurs just after deep meditation when a lucid inner vision quickly clouds over on consciousness turning outward into the physical World. It is usually due to the ego mind overlaying the depths with some superficial and personal preoccupation so that, while the realisation of some important inner sight is recognised, its significance slips back behind the veil of the unconscious.

As if to emphasise Moses's humanity, legend tells us that he asked the Lord, in the Tent of Meeting just outside the camp, the reason for delay. The reply was that now Moses would see why he was not allowed to participate in the construction. The Israelites had supplied the materials and labour, Bezalel and his artisans the form and now he, Moses, would complete the three levels by assembling the Tabernacle through the creative power of the Spirit. Moses said he had no idea how to set about it. The fortieth chapter of Exodus contains his instructions and legend describes how they were implemented.

Moses was told to assemble the Tabernacle according to the law of the four Worlds as indicated by the recurring number forty in the scripture. Firstly he was to set up the Tent of the Tabernacle, put the Ark of the Tokens in it and screen the Ark with the Veil. He was then to bring in the Table and lay it, after which the Lamp-standard was to be brought in. The sequence of instruction would then proceed to unfold, stage by stage, until the Tabernacle was complete with all its furniture and tools within the erected outer Court.

The oral tradition says that, as the day of the assembling of the Tabernacle and its consecration approached, everyone prepared themselves as they had for the receiving of the Decalogue from the

Holy Mountain. The difference here, however, was that the event was going to take place below in the sight of all the people. Moses, therefore, had to prepare himself for the difficult task of being the agent down through which would flow the Divine Will in an act of miraculous creation. In this demonstration the Israelites would witness one of the most profound ideas in the Tradition; that man, the image of God, was the only creature capable of receiving and imparting the Will of the Divine while spanning all four Worlds. This was the purpose of a human being. No other creature, however large and powerful, in the upper or lower Worlds could perform this function.

On the first day of the month of Nison, at the time appointed by the Lord, everyone gathered in the camp before the spread-out components of the Tabernacle. Moses, in a state of balanced equilibrium in which all four levels within him were integrated by his own merit and the help of Grace, approached the scattered parts and touched them according to the order he had been given. At that moment, the Universe aligned throughout and fusion took place above and below as the power flowed down the Worlds through Moses and into the parts of the Tabernacle. They began to move together and to join one another before the amazed eyes of the Children of Israel. The walls of the Tabernacle tenoned and socketed themselves creating, forming and making the sacred spaces of the Sanctuary and the Holy of Holies. Then the great curtains of blue, purple and red cast themselves over the structure before being covered themselves by the three layers of skins. The Ark placed itself within the Holy of Holies and the Veil drew itself across the door, after which the Sanctuary furniture positioned itself and the holy utensils found their places before the screen hung itself over the door. Outside, the Altar took up its position in front of the Tent with the Laver siting itself before the whole complex in the space of the outer Court. Suddenly, everything in and about the Tabernacle was in its proper place. At last the Divine Will to have a Tabernacle throughout all Existence was now manifest in every World.

All that was needed to complete the operation was a ceremony of consecration that would join its purpose with that of man. Thus as Adam, the microcosmic image of the Divine, would serve God within the macrocosmic image of the Tabernacle, Face would begin to behold Face.

After Moses had anointed the Tabernacle and everything in it with oil to symbolise the blessing of Grace, he consecrated the Altar and Laver in the Court, omitting the outer Court for it was not considered

Holy. He then had Aaron and his sons come to the door of the Tent of the Presence and wash themselves so as to be fit to enter the priesthood. Aaron was then ceremonially clothed in the vestments of the High Priest and anointed, after which his sons were dressed and anointed as priests. These rituals of dedication and consecration were completed by the raising of the outer fence and the closing of its gate which separated the sacred from the profane.

At this moment of completion, the Cloud that had accompanied the Israelites from Egypt descended and covered the Tent of Meeting. The Hebrew text says,

'*Uchvod YAHVEH malay et ha Mishkan.*'
'And the Glory Of YAHVEH filled the Tabernacle.'

That is, the Presence of the Divine World manifested throughout all the Worlds to focus within the Tabernacle as it lay under the Cloud of the Holy Spirit. 'And Moses was not able to enter the Tent of Meeting because the Cloud dwelt upon it and the Glory of the Lord filled the Tabernacle'.

According to legend, the descent of the Glory had not occurred on the Earth since the days before Adam and Eve had sinned. On this day, however, it was seen by all the Children of Israel, that is by ordinary men and women as they stood in awe witnessing the outward downflow of Creation touch Earth, then turn upwards in the ascent of inward Evolution.

It was a momentous moment in the cycle of Existence. From this day on there were beings who could perceive Divinity at the mineral, vegetable, animal and human levels of reality. Legend adds that from this day on, the Lord's relationship changed with Moses. He was to hear the Divine voice change from awesome tones of Judgement to a sweet and gentle whisper that spoke more of Mercy. This latter attribute, it is said, permeated all the Worlds that day so that even the demonic forces of the Universe were quietened. The Work of Unification had entered a new phase.

For the individual, all the foregoing describes a profound moment of integration. Suddenly, one day, all that has been learned and practised becomes real. Months and perhaps years of work and preparation coalesce in a deep experience during a ceremony of dedication. In that moment of initiation, everything is brought into unison to make the interior Tabernacle operational. Into this Sanctuary comes a Light that illuminates partially-understood concepts and activates incomplete functions. Suddenly, many separated elements within the being are perceived to form a single inner organism where the Spirit flowing down from the World of Creation can be received and imparted and an individual can act as host and High Priest in his own Holy of Holies to the Presence of the Divine.

The Book of Exodus closes with a verse that describes, in allegory, the situation of a consecrated person who is, from that time, on his way back to the Promised Land, 'For the cloud of the Lord was upon the Tabernacle by day and fire was on it by night, in the sight of all the House of Israel, throughout all their journeys'.

Epilogue

The journey through the Wilderness was to take forty years, or a complete cycle of physical, psychological, spiritual and Divine experience, in which the Israelites were to undergo a total transformation. During this time, they were trained and tested in the gradual process of assimilating the Teaching given to them.

The regular training programme was implemented by the weekly, monthly and annual cycles of the Sabbath and the festivals. This built up a backbone of laws and customs (one camp site was actually called *Ezion-Geber* or 'backbone') which gave a discipline and dignity to the new nation that was to emerge out of the old slave-minded psychology. The parallel in the individual is the long years of training after the initial commitment to spiritual work. Consent is not enough. One has to carry out the Covenant and be tested under the most difficult conditions, which the Wilderness represents, in order to be proved.

The tests came in many forms. The most obvious were the external battles with the peoples who blocked the Israelites' way. These happened as the Israelites crossed frontiers or intruded into different kingdoms. Similarly violent episodes are experienced by a traveller on the spiritual journey as he encounters powerful psychological domains that seek to impede his path or even destroy his developing integrity, as symbolised by the slow integration of the Israelite community with the Tabernacle at its centre. The most dangerous tests came from within in a series of rebellions at different levels. Besides the periodic resistance to the tough conditions of the desert, by still egocentric people who could not yet perceive beyond the immediate situation, there was the insurrection of Korah and the two men, Dathan and Abiram, who had been stopped from quarrelling in Egypt by Moses. This opposition caused a serious schism within the Nation and resulted in the death of many who joined in the confrontation. Such moments occur in spiritual growth when a whole set of concepts or emotional complexes have to be shed or they will destroy years of work. It also occurs in group activities when some members with a little knowledge break from the source and set up on their own, often to stagnate or even die in their pride and belief that only they have the truth or authority. Religious history has many such examples.

Perhaps the most dramatic inner test was symbolised by the claim of Moses's own sister and brother to be his equal before the Lord. They were severely taken to task by the Divine who punished Miriam, the lesser principle of ego, for assuming the initiative against Moses. The psychic gifts of Miriam or Yesod might have clarity, and formal ritual represented by Aaron at Hod may appear to have weight, but these are dependent upon what is imparted by Grace from above, through the elevated level of Moses at the self and his normal position at Nezah or prophecy. Miriam was kept outside the camp in a leprous state of disease until she had learnt her lesson. This phenomenon occurs with people who abuse what occult powers they may have acquired and consider themselves as masters. Many incidents during the latter time in the Wilderness illustrate, in analogue, the problems confronting people well along the inward path. The seduction of the over-confident Israelites by their friendly neighbours' women and culture becomes a major threat to the purity of the people and its belief in the Unity of God. The attempted assault by alien kings who wish to utilise the magic of Balaam, the powerful dark magician, reveals the first contact with real evil that is only encountered beyond a certain point in spiritual development. The incident of Moses's transgression at Kadesh (Numbers 20), in which he made water gush forth by his will and not the Divine's, demonstrates the highest temptation. This fatal mistake can and did cost him the refusal of entry into the Promised Land.

By the time the Israelites finally came to the point of entering Canaan, all but two of those born in Egypt were dead. These survivors were Joshua the Deliverer and Caleb, meaning 'Valiant'. These two had been the only optimistic members of the spying expedition (Numbers 13) into the Holy Land that had caused the original Israelites to be turned back into the desert because of their lack of courage when faced with difficulties. Thus it was that a totally new generation, brought up in the Wilderness under the Torah, crossed the second watery division of the Jordan which symbolised, again, a point of no return. This ends the phase of the Mosaic cycle.

The rest of the Old Testament is concerned with the establishment of the Israelites in the Land flowing with milk and honey. This process is set out in the fierce wars of the Lord, in which not only are the false gods that inhabit the Land of the Spirit destroyed but the unity of the tribes is tested under a set of conditions quite different from the desert.

At this cosmic level, the situation and forces arrayed are totally other than the lower World of the psyche. After many years of struggle under various judges who just about held the Israelites together, the tribes were outwardly unified under Saul whose faults revealed the dangers of being under a human overlord. David, meaning the 'Beloved of God', and the people brought the country, despite his imperfections, to the level of having a central capital or place where the second great Tabernacle of the Temple was built by his son Solomon whose name means peace and completion. Alas, this great and wise king, who, legend says, knew three Worlds, fell from grace because, in his over-confidence and excessive tolerance, he allowed the integrity of the Holy Land to be adulterated. This theme is repeated throughout the Old Testament and in the New, as the people chosen to demonstrate the purpose of Existence periodically reached the highest level and then fell because of neglect of the Teaching. This situation still pertains today at the national and individual level.

What we have been studying together is everyman's *Pilgrim's Progress*. The journey from the beginning of time through all the Worlds and its stages is set out so that whatever level one is at, the Bible will make profound sense and give wise advice. This is possible because the people who composed the original scriptures were fully aware of what and why they were writing. The Bible is possibly one of the most widely read of books. Why? Because it contains the Teaching about God, the Universe and Man, although most people only dimly sense the deep content, despite its human discrepancies, of Beauty and Truth. These esoteric depths may be known only when the seven levels within oneself have been experienced personally. To do this requires the key of inner knowledge or the scriptures will be no more than a hint of other Worlds beyond a hidden door. 'Seek', said one great rabbi, 'and you shall find. Knock and it shall be opened'.

Hear O Israel. The Lord is our God, The Lord is One.

Glossary of Kabbalistic Terms

Asiyyah:	Natural World of Making
AYIN:	Absolute NO-THING
Azilut:	Divine World of Emanation
Beriah:	World of Creation and Spirit
Binah:	Sefirah of Understanding
Daat:	Non-Sefirah of Knowledge
Ego:	Ordinary mind of Yesod
EN SOF:	Absolute ALL
Gevurah:	Sefirah of Judgement
Hesed:	Sefirah of Mercy
Hod:	Sefirah of Reverberation
Hokhmah:	Sefirah of Wisdom
Israel:	Spiritual level of mankind
Keter:	Sefirah of the Crown
Malkhut:	Sefirah of the Kingdom
Menorah:	Seven-branched candle-stand
Merkabah:	Chariot of World of Formation
Metatron:	Archangel of Presence. Enoch translated
Nezah:	Sefirah of Eternity
Sefirah:	Light or Divine principle of the Tree
Shekhinah:	The Divine Presence
Shetiyah:	Foundation Stone of the World
Talmud:	Oral commentaries, laws and folklore on the Bible
Tiferet:	Sefirah of Beauty
Yesod:	Sefirah of Foundation
Yezirah:	World of Formation

Index

A

Aaron, 48, 65, 67, 140, 164
Abraham, 39, 119
Abyss, 153, 194
Adam, xv, 21, 27, 54
Adam Kadmon, 19–25
Adultery, 123
Aholiab, 168, 208, 213
Alphabet, 142, 169
Altar, 150, 221
Amalekites, 105–108
Amram, 48
Angels, 133, 195
Anointing, 221
Ark, 141, 211
Ascension, 50, 132, 195
Assembly of Tabernacle, 222
Aura, 199

B

Balaam, 49, 53, 74, 175, 225
Bezalel, 168, 206, 211
Blood, 77
Book of Covenant, 125–127
Books of Life and Death, 188
Boundaries, 114, 117
Breaking law, 171
Breast-plate, 160–161, 215
Building sequence, 208
Bull, 164
Burnt offering, 150

C

Caleb, 186, 225
Camp, 139
Canaan, 40, 43
Cherubim, 142
Children of Israel, 113
Chosen people, 125
Clairaudience, 189
Clarity, 125
Cleansing, 183
Cloud, 116, 132
Colours, 137
Commandments, 119, 141
Commitment, 114
Company of Blessed, 97
Corruption, 181
Court, 157
Covenant, 58, 64, 197
Coveting, 123
Curtains, 146, 208

D

Dathan and Abiram, 50, 224
David, 226
Desert, 57, 197
Divine voice, 222
Divine ways, 193–194
Divine world, 21
Divine wrath, 179
Doubt, 62, 103

E

Eden, 21, 60
Ego, 102
Egypt, 43, 48, 71
Egyptian scribes, 71
Elders, 67, 96, 102, 109, 114, 130, 132, 176, 177
Elijah, 129, 195
Elim, 96
End of Days, 21, 188
Enoch, 35, 54, 60, 129
Ephod, 160, 215
Ephraimites, 85
Esau, 39, 105
Ethiopia, 53
Eve, 21
Evolution, 210
Ezekiel, 25, 158, 162

F

Faith, 220
Fall, 117, 131
False witness, 123
Father and mother, 122
Five gardens, 147
Fleshpots, 97
Forgetting, 134, 220
Forty days and nights, 198
Free will, 21, 100

G

Gabriel, 192
Genesis, 35–42
Giving, 137, 205
Glory, 19, 194, 195, 199
Gold, 141
Golden Calf, 177, 179, 183
Grace, 49, 59, 62, 67, 96, 98, 189, 194
Guide, 193

H

Hayyah, 171
Healing, 197
Heaven, 129, 132
Hierarchy, 212
High Priests, 157, 159
High Priests' vestments, 160–163
Holy animals, 113, 177
Holy ground, 59
Holy of Holies, 147, 151, 211
Holy Spirit, 192
Holy writ, 164
Horeb, 59, 102
House of Israel, 113, 157
Hur, 108, 168, 176

I

Ignorance, 102
Images, 120, 147
Incense, 167
Inspiration, 206
Isaac, 39
Israel in Egypt, 43

J

Jacob, 39, 40, 105
Jacob's pillow, 194
Jethro, 53, 54, 59, 66, 109
Job, 54
Joseph, 40, 43, 54
Joshua, 107, 181, 192
Just men, 186

K

Kabbalah, 201
Karma, 188, 194
Killing, 122

L

Laver, 150, 212
Levites, 48, 139, 158
Light, 19, 194
Lord's side, 184
Lower halls, 195
Loyalty, 139

M

Magic, 76, 80, 166, 175, 189
Manna, 98, 100
Marah, 95
Marriage, 55, 171
Masons, 212
Massah, 103
Materials, 137
Melchizedek, xv, 36
Menorah, 143, 212
Mercy seat, 142, 212
Meribah, 103
Merit, 195
Metals, 137
Metatron, 60, 129
Michael, 59, 88, 132
Midian, 50, 109
Miracles, 67, 74, 81, 108, 197
Miriam, 48, 103, 225
Miriam's well, 103
Mirror of Existence, 19, 210
Mishkan, 140, 222
Mistakes, 131, 225

Mixed multitude, 175, 183
Mount of God, 59, 67, 195
Murder, 122

N

Name, 59, 193
Names of God, 36, 49, 54, 64, 72, 105, 119
Nile, 77
Noah, 35, 54
Nobles of Israel, 130, 177, 206

O

Occult powers, 189
Offerings, 165
Oracle, 161
Oral Law, xv, 133, 169
Ornaments, 206

P

Pardes, xvi
Passover, 82
Patience, 217
Patriarchs, 181
Payment, 167
Pharaoh, 50, 71–82, 87
Pharaoh's daughter, 48
Physical body, 27
Pillar of fire and cloud, 86
Plagues, 76
Priests, 117, 139, 157, 165
Priestly code, 157, 164, 198
Providence, 55, 77, 98, 194, 209
Psyche, 29
Punishment, 193

Q

Quails, 100

R

Rachel, 39
Radiance, 198
Rams, 146
Raziel, xv, 133, 142
Red Sea, 86, 88, 177
Reincarnation, 120
Rephidim, 102, 105
Resistance, 66
Revelation, 205
Reward, 193
Rock of Shetiyah, 194, 196
Rod and staff of God, 54, 67, 74, 88, 102

S

Sabbath, 100, 122, 170
Sacred places, 209
Sacred weapons, 189
Safeguards, 196
Sanctuary, 147
Satan, 175
Screen, 147
Scribes, 158
Seat of Solomon, 25, 184
Sefirot, 19
Self-destruction, 178
Seven earths and heavens, 121
Seven psychological stages, 195
Severity, 184
Sex, 114, 171
Sheep, 57
Shekhinah, 140, 142, 147
Shem, 36, 54
Shem Ha Meforash, 161, 216
Shining face, 199
Short cuts, 209
Short route, 86
Shur, Wilderness, 95
Sin, Wilderness, 97
Sin, 186
Sinai, 113
Solomon, 226
Solomon's Temple, 194
Solstice, 113
Stealing, 123
Strange fire, 131
Strictness, 183

T

Tabernacle, 146–149
Tabernacle site, 140
Table of Showbread, 143, 212
Tablets of Commandments, 134, 172, 181, 195
Talents, 206
Talmud, xv, 140
Teaching method, 201
Temperaments, four, 139
Tempting and testing God, 103
Tent of meeting, 189, 192
Teshuvah, redemption, 85, 183
Tests, 195
Thirteen attributes of mercy, 196, 198
Thorn bush, burning bush, 59
Thou and I, 39, 65, 192
Throne of Heaven, 133, 142
Timing, 217
Torah, xv, 133
Treasure of God, 115
Tribes, 139, 212
Trust, 100

Truth, 96
Turban, 216
Turning, 181

U

Unification, Work of, 131, 168, 171, 201, 214, 220
Unity of existence, 141
Upper halls, 195
Urim and Thummim, 161

V

Veil before ark, 147
Veil before Moses' face, 199
Violence, 185
Visions, 60, 130, 131
Visit sin, 188

W

Wealth, 214
Will, divine, 19, 27, 54, 76, 141, 221
Work, 209, 214, 216, 219
Written law, 133

Z

Zipporah, 54, 67
Zodiac, 107, 139
Zohar, xvi

www.ingramcontent.com/pod-product-compliance
Lightning Source LLC
Chambersburg PA
CBHW072049110526
44590CB00018B/3102